LOVE FOR THE FAMILY

قُل لَّا أَسْأَلُكُمْ عَلَيْهِ أَجْرًا إِلَّا الْمَوَدَّةَ فِي الْقُرْبَىٰ

"*Say: 'No reward do I ask of you for this except love for the near of kin...'*" Quran, Sūrah al-Shūrā' (42), Verse 23

Included in this Book:
Ziyārah of the Seven Ḥadīth of Imam ʿAlī ibn Mūsā al-Riḍā
Ziyārah of Lady Fāṭima Maʿṣumā bint Mūsā ibn Jaʿfar
Ziyārah of Lady Zaynab bint ʿAlī
Ziyārah of Lady Sakīna bint Ḥusayn
Ziyārat Āle Yāsīn
Munājāt al-Manẓūmah of Imam ʿAlī

Original Translations by
Yasin T. Al-Jibouri, Saleem Bhimji, and Others

Compiled by Saleem Bhimji
Edited by Arifa Hudda

ISBN: 978-1-927930-54-0

Love for the Family
Original Translations by Yasin T. Al-Jibouri, Saleem Bhimji, and Others
Compiled by Saleem Bhimji
Edited by Arifa Hudda

Cover Design and Layout by Saleem Bhimji

Published by Islamic Publishing House
www.iph.ca · iph@iph.ca

Contents

DEDICATION

This book is dedicated to Prophet Muḥammad ﷺ and his immaculate family, the Ahlul Bayt (ʿa) - the pious and self-sacrificing role models who showed us how to truly worship Allah (ʿazza wa jall), live honourable lives, and serve all of humanity. May their celestial light continue to shine and illuminate the path, and help us reach Allah (ʿazza wa jall).

إِنَّا لِلَّٰهِ وَإِنَّا إِلَيْهِ رَاجِعُونَ

IN LOVING MEMORY OF
SULTANALI HUDDA

This book, *Love for the Family*, has been published for the departed soul of Marhoom Sultanali Hudda.

Born: January 8, 1947

Died: December 31, 2024

Marhoom Sultanali Hudda was a beloved son, brother, husband, father, uncle, grandfather, and great-grandfather.

He loved people very much, especially children; and all who had been fortunate enough to know him, had great respect for him. Some took him as a second father, a dear grandfather, or a beloved uncle.

He worked tirelessly his entire life to serve and help those in need; and build a sense of community in Kitchener-Waterloo, Canada, where he lived for more than 50 years.

He had great love in his heart for Prophet Muḥammad ﷺ, and the Ahlul Bayt ؑ. The last trip he took in his life was to Iraq for *ziyārah* of the noble personalities buried there.

He had a heart of gold and will be immensely missed.

Please recite Surah al-Fatiha for his departed soul, and all of the Marhoomeen.

Introduction

In the Name of Allah, the
All-Merciful, the All-Compassionate

In the tapestry of Islamic Spirituality, few threads are as vibrant and enduring as the love for the family of Prophet Muḥammad ﷺ - the Ahlul Bayt عليهم السلام. This love, deeply rooted in the Quranic injunction and the *aḥādīth* from the final Messenger ﷺ, finds one of its most profound expressions in the practice of *ziyārah* - a visitation to the shrines of the Ahlul Bayt عليهم السلام - specific members of the household of the Prophet ﷺ, and other venerated figures in Islamic history.

This book, *Love for the Family,* is more than just a title; it is a declaration of devotion, a commitment to spiritual growth, and an exploration of one of the most cherished practices in Islamic tradition. This book serves as a guide to *ziyārah*, offering both the novice and the experienced pilgrim a deeper understanding of its significance, etiquette, and transformative power.

The concept of *ziyārah* transcends mere physical visitation. It is a spiritual journey that connects a believer with the legacy of Prophet Muḥammad ﷺ and his immaculate family عليهم السلام, allowing one to draw inspiration from their exemplary lives, seek their intercession, and strengthen the bonds of love that tie the Muslim community to its spiritual leaders. Through *ziyārah*, we not only honour the memory of these noble souls but also seek to embody the virtues they exemplified into our own lives.

As you embark on this literary pilgrimage through the pages of this book, you will discover the multifaceted nature of *ziyārah*.

We begin by exploring its fundamental meaning, and the critical importance it holds in Islamic Spirituality.

The necessity of *ziyārah* is not just a matter of religious obligation, but a means of spiritual nourishment and moral upliftment. By understanding the true purpose of *ziyārah*, readers will be better equipped to approach this sacred act with the reverence and sincerity that it deserves.

One of the unique aspects of this book is the introduction and its detailed exploration of the true form of *ziyārah*. Far from being a simple act of visitation, *ziyārah* involves a series of carefully prescribed steps, each imbued with deep spiritual significance. From purification by means of a *ghusl* to the final act of charity upon leaving the sacred shrine, every aspect of *ziyārah* is an opportunity for internal growth and reflection.

The first section of this book meticulously outlines 20 essential elements of proper *ziyārah* etiquette. These range from practical considerations like wearing clean clothes and seeking permission to enter, to more esoteric practices such as the presence of heart and sincere repentance to Allah ﷻ. By adhering to these guidelines, pilgrims can ensure that their *ziyārah* is not only outwardly correct, but inwardly transformative.

Central to this work are the specific *ziyārah* actions and recitations for several key figures in the lineage of the

Prophet's family ﷺ. We delve into the spiritual connections with the eighth Imam, ʿAlī ibn Mūsā al-Riḍā ؑ; his beloved sister, Lady Fāṭima Maʿṣūma bint Mūsā ibn Jaʿfar ؑ; Lady Zaynab bint ʿAlī ؑ; and Lady Sakīna bint Ḥusayn ؑ. Each section introduces these revered personalities, offering insights into their historical significance and spiritual stature, followed by their *ziyārah*: the complete Arabic text of the visitation, along with a clear and easy to understand English translation.

This book does not contain the *ziyārāt* of the various shrines located throughout Iraq, nor other shrines dedicated to the family of the Prophet ﷺ buried throughout Iran, or Arabia. The non-inclusion of the burial sites of these pious personalities should not be seen as a matter of disrespect to them; rather, as there are countless shrines in these various places dedicated to the family of the Prophet ﷺ, as well as respectable companions, and friends of Allah ﷻ *(Awliyāʾ)*, we realized that it would be impossible for us to do justice to their legacy in this work. Although there are numerous shrines within Iran that the faithful visit, however, the two most 'important and prominent ones' are that of the 8th Imam, ʿAlī ibn Mūsā al-Riḍā ؑ, and his sister, Lady Fāṭima Maʿṣūma ؑ.

There are other comprehensive works that have been published, such as ones by Al-Kisa Foundation (www.alkisafoundation.org) which offer beautiful full-colour glimpses into all of the visitations in Iraq and Iran; and we highly recommend readers to purchase those books for their spiritual trips to these sacred places.

The inclusion of *Ziyārat Āle Yāsīn* for the 12th Imam, Al-Ḥujjah ibn Ḥasan al-Mahdī ؑ, adds a unique dimension to this guide, connecting the practice of *ziyārah* to the eschatological hopes of the Muslim community. This *ziyārah* serves as a bridge between the present and the future, allowing believers to express their longing for justice and spiritual renewal that the awaited Imam عجل الله تعالى فرجه الشريف symbolizes.

Love for the Family also recognizes the deeply personal and emotional aspect of *ziyārah* through the inclusion of *Munājāt al-Manẓūmah* - The Versified Whispered Prayer. This beautiful supplication, presented in both its original Arabic and English translation, offers readers a poetic means of expressing their devotion and seeking Divine nearness through the medium of the Prophet's family ﷺ.

Throughout this book, while carefully reading the English translation of each *ziyārah*, readers will find that visitation is not just about following a set of rituals. Rather, it is about cultivating a state of heart and mind that is receptive to spiritual blessings. The emphasis on the presence of heart, humility, and sincere repentance underscores the transformative potential of *ziyārah*. It is an act that, when performed with true understanding and devotion, can lead to profound personal growth and a deeper connection with the Divine.

Moreover, *Love for the Family* situates the practice of *ziyārah* within the broader context of Islamic Spirituality and Ethics. The emphasis on helping the needy and showing respect to volunteers at the shrines reminds us that love for the Prophet's family ﷺ must be expressed not just through rituals, but through embodying their values into our daily lives.

As you journey through these pages, you will find that *ziyārah* is a multifaceted gem, reflecting different aspects of

Islamic Spirituality. It is an act of remembrance, a means of seeking intercession, a method of moral and spiritual education, and a way of strengthening the bonds of community among believers.

This book is more than just a manual; it is an invitation to deepen one's love for the Prophet's family ﷷ, and by extension, one's love for Allah ﷻ and His Messenger ﷺ. It challenges readers to move beyond superficial understandings of religious practices and engage with their faith at a profound level.

Whether you are preparing for a physical journey to these sacred sites or seeking to perform a spiritual *ziyārah* from your home, this book will serve as an indispensable companion. It offers not just instructions, but insights; not just rituals, but reflections - guiding you towards a more meaningful and transformative experience of *ziyārah*.

As we conclude this introduction, it is our sincere hope that *Love for the Family* will kindle or rekindle in your heart a deep and abiding love for the Ahlul Bayt ﷷ. May this book be a means of drawing closer to their exemplary legacy; and through them, to the Divine presence. In the end, true love for the family of the Prophet ﷷ is nothing less than an expression of love for Allah ﷻ and His Messenger ﷺ - a love that has the power to transform hearts, uplift spirits, and illuminate the path to spiritual excellence.

The title of this book, *Love for the Family*, is a direct reference to Verse 23 of Sūrah al-Shūrā (Chapter 42) in which the Noble Prophet ﷺ was ordered by Allah ﷻ to proclaim that in return for his lifetime of challenges, grief, and anxiety to convey the teachings of Islam, the Quran, that he ask for no reward except **Love for his Family**: *"Say: 'No reward do I ask of you for this except the love of those near of kin.'"*[1]

Based on this verse, and the commentaries offered by the scholars of Islam, we see that in the vast tapestry of Divine wisdom, Allah's ﷻ tidings unfold like a celestial garden, and its blossoms of mercy and compassion stretch beyond the horizons of human comprehension. Allah ﷻ, in His infinite Grace, has illuminated the path of righteousness for His devoted servants, marking it with the twin beacons of faith and virtuous deeds - which have been taught to the believers through the two weighty things: the Quran and the Ahlul Bayt (عليهم السلام).

At the heart of our spiritual journey lies a profound truth which must be displayed openly: Love for the Prophet's ﷺ blessed family, the Ahlul Bayt (عليهم السلام). This love is not merely a sentimental feeling; rather, it must be a transformative force that changes the human soul. It must be a love that transcends the boundaries of the physical world, reaching the essence of creation.

The final Messenger of Allah ﷻ, the beloved Prophet Muḥammad ﷺ - a beacon of light in the darkness of ignorance - was commanded by the Almighty to invite all of those who would follow him to this love. His call echoes for over the past 1,400 years: "I ask from you NO reward except love for my near kin." These words - simple, yet profound -

---

[1] Quran, Sūrah al-Shūrā (42), Verse 23.

﴿...قُل لَّا أَسْأَلُكُمْ عَلَيْهِ أَجْرًا إِلَّا الْمَوَدَّةَ فِي الْقُرْبَىٰ...﴾

unlock the gates to truly appreciate his efforts and 'paying' him back for his tireless efforts.

This love - pure and unadulterated - reflects the love we must have for Allah ﷻ Himself. The heart that loves the Ahlul Bayt ﷺ will naturally reflect the beauty of Divine Attributes, becoming a vessel for wisdom, and a channel of Grace from the Almighty.

The Ahlul Bayt ﷺ - those purified souls chosen by Allah ﷻ Himself - stand as beacons of immaculate character in their words and deeds. Their light, emanating from the same source as the Prophetic radiance, guides the seekers through the darkest times. To love them is to love perfection itself. This sacred love cannot remain passive, it must be an active force - a spiritual current that propels a believer towards acts of piety.

As a seeker traverses this path of love, one will find oneself enveloped in a mantle of Divine Forgiveness. The veils of separation will become lifted, revealing glimpses of a reality beyond the confines of mortal perception. In loving the Ahlul Bayt ﷺ, a servant will draw closer to the Beloved, and one's heart will become a sanctuary of peace and Divine presence.

This love, when embraced in its totality, will become a comprehensive system of spiritual ascension. It is a rope extended from the heavens, offering salvation to those who grasp it with sincerity. Through this love, the Quran will be better understood, and the essence of the Prophetic mission will be preserved for generations to come.

However, one needs to know: Who are the "near of kin" that the final Messenger, Prophet Muḥammad ﷺ was referring to? This is a question which countless individuals have inquired about, and many have sought to define it through their own lens. Some have included people within the ranks that Allah ﷻ and His Prophet ﷺ have not endorsed.

For the Shīʿas, our understanding of the Quran can only come from the legitimate interpreters of this Divine Book - namely the Ahlul Bayt ‎(ع)‎ - however here, we refer to a famous scholar of the Ahlul Sunnah, Imam al-Ṭabarānī, in his work, *Muʿjam al-Ṭabarānī al-Kabīr,* who quotes the following *ḥadīth*:

> "...From Ibn ʿAbbās, may Allah be pleased with them both, in which he said: "When the verse: '*Say: No reward do I ask of you for this except love for the near of kin,*' was revealed, we said: 'O Messenger of Allah! And who are 'the near of kin' - those upon whom having love for is an obligation?' He (the final Prophet ﷺ) replied: **'They are ʿAlī, Fāṭima, and their children.'"**[2]

---

[2] Suyūṭī, Jalāl al-Dīn, *Al-Durr al-Manthūr,* Vol. 6, Pg. 7, in which he said: "Ibn al-Mundhir, Ibn Abī Hātim, at-Tabarānī, and Ibn Mardawayh reported through the chain of Saʿid ibn Jubayr, from Ibn ʿAbbās..."

This has also been narrated by Ibn Mardawayh as mentioned in *Fatḥ al-Qadīr* in Vol. 4, Pg. 536; *Rūḥ al-Maʿānī* in Vol. 25, Pg. 29; *Kashf al-Ghummah* in Vol. 1, Pg. 324; and *Kashf al-Yaqīn* on Pg. 398.

At the end of this *ḥadīth* in the latter two sources, it states: "He said it three times," and in both of them "their two sons" was mentioned instead of "their two children."

Al-Zamakhsharī narrates it in his *Tafsīr al-Kashshāf* in Vol. 3, Pg. 402 that: "It is reported that when this was revealed, it was asked: 'O Messenger of Allah, who are these relatives of yours whose love has become obligatory upon us?' He replied: "ʿAlī, Fāṭima, and their two sons.'"

In addition, a Sunnī commentator of the Quran, al-Zamakhsharī, in his seminal work, *Tafsīr al-Kashshāf,* quotes the below *ḥadīth* in relation to this verse:

> "Indeed, the one who dies while on the love for the family of Muḥammad has died as a martyr *(shahīd)*; and indeed, the one who dies while on the love for the family of Muḥammad has died being forgiven [of all of their sins]; and indeed, the one who dies while on the love for the family of Muḥammad has died as one who has turned back [to Allah in repentance]; and indeed, the one who dies while on the love for the family of Muḥammad has died as a believer with their faith perfected; and indeed, the one who dies while on the love for the family of Muḥammad has died as one who will be given the glad tidings by the Angel of Death for having attained Paradise, and then [the angels] Munkir and Nakīr; and indeed, the one who dies while on the love for the family of Muḥammad will be escorted into

---

From him, Fakhr al-Rāzī also narrated a similar thing it in his *tafsīr, Tafsīr al-Kabīr,* in Vol. 27, Pg. 166.

Abu Ḥayyān al-Andalūsī narrated in his *tafsīr, Tafsīr al-Baḥr al-Muḥīt,* in Vol. 7, Pg. 516, that Ibn ʿAbbās said: "It was asked: 'O Messenger of Allah, who are your relatives whose love you have commanded upon us?' He replied: 'ʿAlī, Fāṭima, and their two sons.'"

Al-Haythamī narrated a similar incident in his *Majmaʿ al-Zawāʾid* in Vol. 9, Pg. 168.

The Arabic text of this *ḥadīth* is as follows:

عن ابن عباس رضي الله تعالى عنهما قال: لما نزلت ﴿قُل لَا أَسْأَلُكُمْ عَلَيْهِ أَجْرًا إِلَّا الْمَوَدَّةَ فِي الْقُرْبَىٰ﴾ قالوا: يا رسول الله ومن قرابتك هؤلاء الذين وجبت علينا مودتهم؟ قال علي وفاطمة وابناهما.

Paradise just as a bride is escorted to the house of her husband; and indeed, the one who dies while on the love for the family of Muḥammad will have two doors which lead towards Paradise opened in their grave; and indeed, the one who dies while on the love for the family of Muḥammad will find that Allah will make their grave as a visiting spot for the Angels of Mercy; and indeed, the one who dies while on the love for the family of Muḥammad has died on the path of the *Sunnah* (the ways of Prophet Muḥammad ﷺ) and *Jamāʿah* (the community of true followers of Prophet Muḥammad ﷺ); and indeed, the one who dies while harbouring hatred for the family of Muḥammad will come on the Day of Resurrection with [the following words] written on their forehead: 'So and so is despondent from the Mercy of Allah' [and will thus be forever prevented from entering into Paradise]; and indeed, the one who dies while harbouring hatred for the family of Muḥammad has died as a disbeliever *(kāfir)*; and indeed, the one who dies while harbouring hatred for the family of Muḥammad shall never smell the fragrance of Paradise..."[3]

---

[3] See *Tafsīr al-Kashshāf* under Sūrah al-Shūrā' (42), Verse 23, Ḥadīth 999. The Arabic text of this is as follows:

مَنْ مَاتَ عَلَىٰ حُبِّ آلِ مُحَمَّدٍ مَاتَ شَهِيدًا، أَلَا وَمَنْ مَاتَ عَلَىٰ حُبِّ آلِ مُحَمَّدٍ مَاتَ مَغْفُورًا لَهُ، أَلَا وَمَنْ مَاتَ عَلَىٰ حُبِّ آلِ مُحَمَّدٍ مَاتَ تَائِبًا، أَلَا وَمَنْ مَاتَ عَلَىٰ حُبِّ آلِ مُحَمَّدٍ مَاتَ مُؤْمِنًا مُسْتَكْمِلَ الْإِيمَانَ، أَلَا وَمَنْ مَاتَ عَلَىٰ حُبِّ آلِ مُحَمَّدٍ مَاتَ بَشَّرَهُ مَلَكُ الْـمَوْتِ بِالْجَنَّةِ، ثُمَّ مُنْكِرٍ وَنَكِيرٍ، أَلَا وَمَنْ مَاتَ عَلَىٰ حُبِّ آلِ مُحَمَّدٍ يَزِفُ إِلَىٰ الْجَنَّةِ كَمَا تَزِفُ الْعُرُوسَ إِلَىٰ بَيْتِ زَوْجِهَا، أَلَا وَمَنْ مَاتَ عَلَىٰ حُبِّ آلِ مُحَمَّدٍ فُتِحَ لَهُ فِي قَبْرِهِ بَابَانِ

As we conclude this introduction, it is with profound gratitude that we acknowledge the many individuals whose contributions have been instrumental in bringing *Love for the Family* to fruition.

This book is not the result of one person's efforts, but rather, a collective labour of love and devotion to Prophet Muhammad ﷺ and his beloved family, the Ahlul Bayt (ʿa) - separated physically - however brought together through their collective *Love for the Family.*

We acknowledge the anonymous individuals who encouraged us to embark on this project and supported its first limited print run overseas.

We are also indebted to Br. Yasin T. Al-Jibouri, whose translation into English has greatly enriched this publication with rendering the *ziyārah* of Lady Sakīna bint Ḥusayn (ʿa).

A special note of appreciation goes to the individual (who wished to remain anonymous) - who provided her English paper research on *The Versified Whispered Prayer (Munājāt al-Manẓūmah)* of Imam ʿAlī (ʿa). Her scholarly insights and desire to see this important work included in our publication added a valuable dimension to this book. Her contribution serves as a testament to the collaborative spirit that underlies this project.

إِلىٰ الْجَنَّةِ، أَلاَ وَمَنْ مَاتَ عَلَىٰ حُبِّ آلِ مُحَمَّدٍ جَعَلَ اللّٰهُ قَبْرَهُ مَزارَ مَلاَئِكَةِ الرَّحْمَةِ، أَلاَ وَمَنْ مَاتَ عَلَىٰ حُبِّ آلِ مُحَمَّدٍ مَاتَ عَلَىٰ السُّنَّةِ وَالْجَمَاعَةِ، أَلاَ وَمَنْ مَاتَ عَلَىٰ بُغْضِ آلِ مُحَمَّدٍ جَآءَ يَوْمَ الْقِيَامَةِ مَكْتُوبٌ بَيْنَ عَيْنَيهِ: آيِسٌ مِنْ رَحْمَةِ اللّٰهِ، أَلاَ وَمَنْ مَاتَ عَلَىٰ بُغْضِ آلِ مُحَمَّدٍ مَاتَ كَافِرًا، أَلاَ وَمَنْ مَاتَ عَلَىٰ بُغْضِ آلِ مُحَمَّدٍ لَمْ يَشُمُّ رَائِحَةَ الْجَنَّةِ...

I cannot overstate my gratitude to our devoted editor, my wife, Sr. Arifa Hudda. For a quarter of a century, she has tirelessly served the cause of the Prophet's family ﷷ through her meticulous review and careful editing of my writings and translations. Her expertise, attention to detail, and deep understanding of the subject matter have been instrumental in refining and elevating the quality of this work.

To these individuals, and any others who supported this project in various ways, such as financially, we offer our sincere thanks. Your contributions - whether large or small, acknowledged or anonymous - have all played a crucial role in bringing this book to fruition. It is our fervent hope that *Love for the Family* will serve as a lasting testament to your dedication, and a means of spreading love and understanding for the revered Ahlul Bayt ﷷ.

May Allah ﷻ reward you all abundantly for your efforts in the service of His beloved Prophet ﷺ and his pure family ﷷ.

In closing, we remind ourselves that all praise belongs to Allah ﷻ alone for all of His assistance and guidance - any mistakes are ours.

We pray that the Almighty ﷻ accepts this humble book, *Love for the Family*, from all of us; and may the **Prophet and his immaculate family, the Ahlul Bayt**, peace and blessings be upon all of them, be pleased with this project.

"Say: 'No reward do I ask of you for this except the love of those near of kin.'"

Quran, Sūrah al-Shūrā (42), Verse 23

Saleem Bhimji

January 14th, 2025 CE

13th of Rajab, 1446 AH

Birth Anniversary of the Commander of the Faithful, Imam ʿAlī ibn Abī Ṭālib

Richmond, British Columbia, Canada

The above calligraphy, read from the bottom right in a clockwise fashion, features the names of the fourteen Maʿṣūmīn - beginning with Prophet Muḥammad al-Muṣṭafā ﷺ and ending with Imam al-Mahdī عجل الله تعالى فرجه الشريف

بسم الله الرحمن الرحيم

In the Name of Allah, the
All-Merciful, the All-Compassionate

Introduction to Ziyārah[4]

Meaning of Ziyārah

The word *ziyārah* is derived from the word *zawr* (زور) which literally means "to repel or turn aside from something."

In Arabic, a lie is called *zūr* because it 'sidetracks from the path of the truth.'

In Chapter 25 (Sūrah al-Furqān), Verse 72 of the Quran, we see this word used in the following context when speaking about the qualities of the Servants of the All-Merciful *('Ibād al-Raḥmān)*: "And (they are) those who do not give false testimony, and when they come upon vain talk, they pass by nobly."[5]

It is also used in the meaning of 'reclining towards

---

[4] The majority of this introduction was summarized and translated from the work entitled, *The Philosophy and Ritual of Pilgrimage (Falsafa-e Ziyārat wa Āiyīn Ān),* written by Shaykh Murtaḍā Jawādī Āmulī with modifications.

[5] The Arabic of this verse is:

﴿وَالَّذِينَ لَا يَشْهَدُونَ الزُّورَ وَإِذَا مَرُّوا بِاللَّغْوِ مَرُّوا كِرَامًا﴾

something' - as can be seen in the Quran in Chapter 18 (Sūrah al-Kahf), Verse 17: "...you may see the sun, when it rises, **slanting** towards the right of their cave; and when it sets, cut across them towards the left..."[6]

The third usage, which relates somewhat to our discussion, is featured in Chapter 102 (Sūrah al-Takāthur), in Verses 1 and 2 in which we are reminded: "Rivalry [and vainglory] distracted you, until **you visited** the graves."[7]

A *zā'ir* (one who is performing the *ziyārah)* is referred to as such because they are drawing away from everyone and everything other than the one whom they expect to visit.

Therefore, the use of the word *ziyārah* for the visiting of the virtuous, devout human beings (usually for those who are no longer alive) is because this act seeks the deflection from the mundane routines of this material world and focuses our attention on the spiritual realms.

In his introduction to the Commentary on *Ziyārat 'Āshūrā'* entitled *The Sacred Effusion*[8] Shaykh Muhammad Khalfan writes: "Our aim of *ziyārah*, however, must transcend seeking personal benefits. It is therefore important to first decipher the purpose of *ziyārah* ... Of course, this does not mean that one should not seek personal benefits from the

---

[6] The Arabic of this verse is:

﴿وَتَرَى الشَّمْسَ إِذَا طَلَعَت تَّزَاوَرُ عَن كَهْفِهِمْ ذَاتَ الْيَمِينِ وَإِذَا غَرَبَت تَّقْرِضُهُمْ ذَاتَ الشِّمَالِ﴾

[7] The Arabic of this verse is:

﴿أَلْهَاكُمُ التَّكَاثُرُ. حَتَّىٰ زُرْتُمُ الْمَقَابِرَ﴾

[8] Volume One can be found at: www.al-islam.org/sacred-effusion-volume-1-muhammad-m-khalfan

great personalities, but one must at least have realized the ultimate purpose of *ziyārah* ..."

Necessity and Importance of Ziyārah

Ziyārah is "a means to establish a connection between the visitor and the one whom they intend to visit, and in the faith of Islam, such a spiritual visit will have a great impact on the visitor."

These people whom we go to great lengths to visit are individuals who hold a great position in the presence of Allah ﷻ, and simply standing in their company entails us to benefit from the spiritual aura which they emanate. In addition, we should be conscious of the fact that while we are in their presence, we are also in the company of the countless angels which are continuously encircling them.

A man narrates the following: "I entered [the city of] Madinah and went to see Abā ʿAbdillāh (Imam Jaʿfar al-Ṣādiq ﷺ) and said to him: 'May I be sacrificed for you! I have come to see you; however, I have not gone to visit [the grave of] the Commander of the Faithful [Imam ʿAlī ibn Abī Ṭālib ﷺ].' Imam Jaʿfar al-Ṣādiq said to me: 'You have done something wrong, and had you not been one of those from amongst our true followers (Shīʿas), I would not have even looked at you! Will you not go and visit the one whom Allah Himself visits, along with the angels, and the one whom the [previous] Prophets even visit, and whom the other true believers also go to visit?" I said to the Imam: "May I be sacrificed for you! How should I have known this?" The Imam replied: "Know that indeed the Commander of the Faithful, in the sight of Allah, is the greatest from among all of the Imams, and he has the reward of all of the good deeds performed [by all of humanity], and in relation to their good deeds are they given stature."[9]

This shows us the importance of performing *ziyārah* - where Allah ﷻ, His angels, and all the previous Prophets ﷺ engage in this great act, then who are we to turn away from visiting such noble personalities!?

However, we should keep in mind that if we do not have the ability to travel to the physical location of the graves, then this does not mean that we should not greet and salute these personalities from whenever we are, or that we should be deprived of such mercies and blessings which Allah ﷻ grants. Rather, we have been told that: "If one of you finds oneself in a distant land, in a faraway home, then let them go to the roof of their house, perform a two *rak'at* prayer, and direct their face towards our resting places as they salute us, for this salutation will reach us. You should greet the Imams from a distance, just as you greet them when you are near them, except it is not proper that you say: 'I have come to you as a visitor,' but rather, you should say in its place: 'I have directed my heart towards you with my *ziyārah*, since I am unable to be at the place of your shrine, and I have

[9] Ḥasan, Muḥammad ibn al-, *Tahdhīb al-Aḥkām*, Vol. 6, Pg. 20. The Arabic text of this tradition is as follows:

دَخَلْتُ الْمَدِينَةَ فَأَتَيْتُ أَبَا عَبْدِ اللّهِ عليه السلام فَقُلْتُ: جُعِلْتُ فِدَاكَ أَتَيْتُكَ وَلَمْ أَزُرْ أَمِيرَ الْمُؤْمِنِينَ عليه السلام. قَالَ: بِئْسَ مَا صَنَعْتَ لَوْ لَا أَنَّكَ مِنْ شِيعَتِنَا مَا نَظَرْتُ إِلَيْكَ أَلَا تَزُورُ مَنْ يَزُورُهُ اللّهُ مَعَ الْمَلَآئِكَةِ وَيَزُورُهُ الْأَنْبِيَآءُ وَيَزُورُهُ الْمُؤْمِنُونَ؟ قُلْتُ: جُعِلْتُ فِدَاكَ مَا عَلِمْتُ ذٰلِكَ؟ قَالَ: إِعْلَمْ أَنَّ أَمِيرَ الْمُؤْمِنِينَ عليه السلام أَفْضَلُ عِنْدَ اللّهِ مِنَ الْأَئِمَّةِ كُلِّهِمْ وَلَهُ ثَوَابُ أَعْمَالِهِمْ وَعَلَىٰ قَدْرِ أَعْمَالِهِمْ فُضِّلُوا.

directed my salutation to you due to my knowledge that it (this salutation) will reach you; Allah blesses you; so, do intercede on my behalf with your Lord, the All-Great, the All-Exalted One,' then you should state your plea as you like."[10]

The Purpose of Ziyārah

What is the ultimate purpose of going for *ziyārah*? Is it just to make the journey of a few hundred or few thousand kilometers to spend a couple of days in a foreign country; to go into an ornate masjid (or in the case of the *ziyārah* in Jannatul Baqīʿ, visiting a 24 hour guarded and secured graveyard encircled by a 20 foot high iron barrier); to recite a few words of salutations and praise - only to leave and then classify oneself as "having done" the *ziyārah* of a particular religious personality - or should it be something greater than this?

One of the fundamental philosophies behind *ziyārah* is to truly **get to know** every aspect of the individual whom we are visiting - whether it be a Prophet, an Imam, or another important personality. Knowing, however, does not mean just to identify their name, their mother's and father's names, their birthplace and resting place, and other such things;

[10] *Tahdhīb al-Aḥkām*, Vol. 6, Pg. 103. The Arabic text of this tradition is as follows:

إِذَا بَعُدَتْ بِأَحَدِكُمُ الشُّقَّةُ وَنَأَتْ بِهِ الدَّارُ فَلْيَعْلُ عَلَىٰ مَنْزِلِهِ وَلْيُصَلِّ رَكْعَتَيْنِ وَلْيَوُمَّ بِالسَّلامِ إِلَىٰ قُبُورِنَا فَإِنَّ ذٰلِكَ يَصِلُ إِلَيْنَا. وَتُسَلِّمُ عَلَىٰ الأَئِمَّةِ ﷺ مِنْ بَعِيدٍ كَمَا تُسَلِّمُ عَلَيْهِمْ مِنْ قَرِيبٍ غَيْرَ أَنَّكَ لَا يَصِحُّ أَنْ تَقُولَ: أَتَيْتُكَ زَائِرًا. بَلْ تَقُولُ فِي مَوْضِعِهِ: قَصَدْتُ بِقَلْبِي زَائِرًا إِذْ عَجَزْتُ عَنْ حُضُورِ مَشْهَدِكَ وَوَجَّهْتُ إِلَيْكَ سَلَامِي لِعِلْمِي بِأَنَّهُ يَبْلُغُكَ صَلَّى اللهُ عَلَيْكَ فَاشْفَعْ لِي عِنْدَ رَبِّكَ جَلَّ وَعَزَّ وَتَدْعُو بِمَا أَحْبَبْتَ.

rather, it means to **truly know** that individual, why they were sent by Allah ﷻ, what their mission and message was, and what they did to uphold it. Through this, we may begin to make an inner change to rectify our character and begin to live up to the ideals which the one whom we are visiting lived and died for.

If *ziyārah* does not have the ability to make a powerful change in our lives, and mold us to stand up in the face of oppression and tyranny and ensure that injustice is never perpetrated on the face of this earth, then so many governments would not have tried to prevent people from visiting these resting places - as we have seen in the history of Syria, Iran, Iraq, and Arabia over the past 1,400 years!

If *ziyārah* was just to travel to their shrines, say "hello" to them, recite a two *rak'at* prayer, then head home, surely for the past 1,400 years, the various empires which have come and gone would not have put so many restrictions on visiting the shrines of the Prophet ﷺ, his noble family ؑ, and their esteemed companions!

If *ziyārah* was just a quick greeting, would it make sense for political rulers to limit the emotions which people show at these public places, or control who can and cannot visit the shrines? Indeed, such governments know that by a person gaining full knowledge of the one whom they are about to visit, and their entire life's struggles, they have the potential in them to bring about a massive internal revolution which has the possibility to spill onto the streets and awaken the masses. It is this Muslim-awakening which the rulers have feared for the past 14 centuries, and even up until today they still tremble at the thought of allowing a free flow of visitors to the shrines and graveyards of such noble individuals.

The permissibility or impermissibility of performing the *ziyārah* has nothing to do with "grave worship" for no one in their right mind worships a grave, or even the person buried in the grave - we only worship Allah ﷻ and direct all our attention towards Him alone!

The True Form of Ziyārah

Every act of worship that Islam has mandated has certain undertakings which are related to it - some are obligatory *(wājib)* and must be performed, while others are recommended *(mustaḥabb)* - and in Islamic terminology, these are referred to as the *'adab'* or courtesies.

For example, before a Muslim begins the daily prayers, they need to ensure that the time has set in, that they have performed the ritual ablution, they are facing the *qiblah*, etc. These are all obligations which need to be fulfilled for the *ṣalāt* to be correct. At the same time, there are a series of recommended actions which one should perform before starting the prayers, such as brushing the teeth, applying perfume, wearing the cleanest of clothes, wearing an *ʿaqīq* ring, etc.

When on the spiritual excursion of *ziyārah* to one of the sacred shrines, we need to try and observe the following 20 points to ensure that we can benefit from the spiritual bounties contained within the trip and gain the utmost of blessings while we are in the presence of the illustrious personalities that we are fortunate to visit.

Please note that what we present here are just the "basics" - each of these points can be elaborated in further detail, however, we will leave the detailed discussions for another time.

1. Ghusl

When going to the sacred shrines, we must realize that we are entering into the presence of individuals who are purified from all filth and uncleanliness, and as such, we too need to ensure that we meet them in a clean state - both physically and spiritually. Since the body is going to enter their sacred homes, and we will be in the company of thousands of other believers, we need to ensure our physical cleanliness by performing a *ghusl.* Once that is complete, then we can also work on our inner purity which can be accomplished by the performance of many actions, such as the actual *ziyārah* of the immaculate ones, and the other noble personalities who we visit. When Imam Jaʿfar al-Ṣādiq ﷺ was asked about the verse of the Quran: "...put on your adornment on every occasion of prayer..."[11] He replied by stating that 'adornment' in this verse means: "[Performance] of a *ghusl* when going to meet every Divinely-appointed guide (Imam)."[12]

---

[11] Quran, Sūrah al-Aʿrāf (7), Verse 31. The Arabic of this is:

﴿...خُذُوا زِينَتَكُمْ عِنْدَ كُلِّ مَسْجِدٍ...﴾

[12] ʿAllāmah al-Majlisī, *Biḥār al-Anwār*, Vol. 97, Pg. 132. The Arabic text of this is as follows:

اَلْغُسْلُ عِنْدَ لِقَاءِ كُلِّ إِمَامٍ

2. Supplications at the Time of Ghusl

Great scholars who have narrated the traditions of the Ahlul Bayt ﷺ, such as Al-Kafʿamī in his book, *Al-Balad al-Amīn,* and Shahīd al-Awwal in his book, *Al-Nafaliyyah,* have presented supplications that we should read when we are performing the *ghusl.* These prayers help us focus on the actions we are about to perform and further strengthen the spiritual connection which we are trying to enhance through the *ziyārah.* For example, one supplication is as follows: "O Allah! Purify my heart and expand my spiritual chest and permit Your praise and thanks to flow from my tongue. O Allah! Make this *(ghusl)* a means of purification, a cure, and a celestial light for me, as indeed You have Power over all things!"[13]

3. Humbleness and Humility

After having made the intention and preparing to proceed towards the sacred shrine, one must display both outward and inward humbleness and humility. One's every physical step from home to the shrine must be made with modesty, and with the thought in mind of the greatness of the individuals whom one is visiting, and by developing calmness, tranquility, and peace in one's heart. One should be preoccupied with uttering the praise of Allah ﷻ and sending salutations to the Prophet ﷺ and his family ﷺ while

---

[13] Kafʿamī, Taqī al-Dīn Ibrāhīm al-, *Al-Balad al-Amīn fil Duriʿ al-Ḥaṣīn,* Pg. 276. The Arabic text of this is as follows:

أَللّٰهُمَّ طَهِّرْ قَلْبِي وَاشْرَحْ لِي صَدْرِي وَأَجْرِ عَلَىٰ لِسَانِي مِدْحَتَكَ وَالثَّنَآءَ عَلَيْكَ. أَللّٰهُمَّ اجْعَلْهُ لِي طَهُورًا وَشِفَآءً وَنُورًا إِنَّكَ عَلَىٰ كُلِّ شَيْءٍ قَدِيرٌ

walking to the shrine.

Through this constant remembrance of the Creator and His chosen guides, and their status and way of life, we will further be able to enhance our own humbleness and realize our own insignificance in relation to their grand station.

In this regards, Imam Jaʿfar al-Ṣādiq ﷺ showed us how to approach the grave of Imam al-Ḥusayn ﷺ in the following words: "When you are going towards Abā ʿAbdillāh, peace be upon him, perform a *ghusl* in the tributary of [the River] Furāt, then put on clean clothes, and walk barefooted, as indeed you are in a sanctuary of the sanctuaries of Allah and of His Messenger. Thus, I advise you to continuously magnify Allah (by reciting أَللّٰهُ أَكْبَرُ); and sanctify Allah (by reciting لَا إِلٰهَ إِلَّا اللّٰهُ); and venerate Allah (by reciting سُبْحَانَ اللّٰهِ); and praise Allah (by reciting أَلْحَمْدُ لِلّٰهِ); and ennoble Allah (by reciting سُبْحَانَ اللّٰهِ رَبِّيَ الْعَظِيمِ), the Glorious and Majestic; and by sending prayers and salutations upon Muḥammad and his family (by reciting *Ṣalawāt*: أَللّٰهُمَّ صَلِّ عَلَىٰ مُحَمَّدٍ وَآلِ مُحَمَّدٍ); and continue in this way until you reach the door of the shrine."[14]

4. Clean Clothes

We need to realize who we are going to visit, so when we enter the presence of such important personalities, we must

[14] *Biḥār al-Anwār*, Vol. 98, Pg. 152. The Arabic text of this is as follows:

إِذَا أَتَيْتَ أَبَا عَبْدِ اللّٰهِ ﷺ فَاغْتَسِلْ عَلَى شَاطِئِ الْفُرَاتِ ثُمَّ الْبَسْ ثِيَابَكَ الطَّاهِرَةَ ثُمَّ امْشِ حَافِيًا فَإِنَّكَ فِي حَرَمٍ مِنْ حَرَمِ اللّٰهِ وَحَرَمِ رَسُولِهِ وَعَلَيْكَ بِالتَّكْبِيرِ وَالتَّهْلِيلِ وَالتَّسْبِيحِ وَالتَّحْمِيدِ وَالتَّعْظِيمِ لِلّٰهِ عَزَّ وَجَلَّ كَثِيرًا وَالصَّلَاةِ عَلَىٰ مُحَمَّدٍ وَأَهْلِ بَيْتِهِ حَتَّى تَصِيرَ إِلَىٰ بَابِ الْحَيْرِ

dress as best as we can - this means wearing nice clean clothes to make ourselves look presentable.

Indeed, it is true that Allah ﷻ does not look at our outward appearance, rather He looks at our hearts; however, we are still obligated to always dress appropriately, and what better time than when we are going to visit such sacred space! In addition, we should ensure that we smell good by perfume, and that there is no smell on our body that could cause any kind of discomfort to others.

5. Permission to Enter

One of the clear Quranic mandates for entering the homes of the Prophet ﷺ is to ask him for permission - and this is done in our age through the recitation of the 'permission to enter' *(idhne dukhūl)* which is often posted at the main entrance of the shrines or found in the books of *Ziyārāt.*

One would never think of walking into a friend's house without knocking on their door or ringing the doorbell; similarly, the way of announcing one's entry into the homes of the beloved Messenger of Allah ﷺ and his family ﷺ is to 'ask for permission' through the recitation of the phrases mentioned in the appropriate books of supplication - keeping in mind that the "homes" of the Messenger ﷺ do not only include his house (and now the Masjid) in Madina, but also the shrines of his beloved family members ﷺ - whether they be in Syria, Egypt, Iraq, Iran, Saudi Arabia, or elsewhere. Allah ﷻ tells us in the Quran: "O you who believe! Do not enter the Prophet's houses unless permission is granted to you for a meal..."[15]

6. Kissing the Sacred Space

As we enter the gates of the shrines, we are recommended to kiss the doorways as a show of respect and veneration for the one whom we are about to meet. In no way can this be equated to worship of the person buried in that area, or worship of the building, or anything of that sort - rather, it is a way to show our respect to the person buried within that area.

Today, when anyone picks up a copy of the Quran, the first thing they do is to kiss the cover of the Noble Book - even though the text is located inside the book and the cover merely "holds" the papers together - yet no one has a problem with this act!

Similarly, kissing the entrance of the shrine is to show reverence to the entire area and the one who is buried there. Imam Jaʿfar al-Ṣādiq ﷺ has been quoted as saying: "Then kiss the entrance of the shrine, and begin to walk with right foot, before the left foot..."[16]

7. Walking

As we walk through the courtyard and make our way to the burial spot, we should enter with our right foot and walk

---

[15] Quran, Sūrah al-Aḥzāb (33), Verse 53. The Arabic of this is:

﴿يَأَيُّهَا الَّذِينَ آمَنُواْ لَا تَدْخُلُواْ بُيُوتَ النَّبِيِّ إِلَّا أَن يُؤْذَنَ لَكُمْ إِلَىٰ طَعَامٍ...﴾

[16] *Biḥār al-Anwār*, Vol. 97, Pg. 284. The Arabic text of this is as follows:

ثُمَّ قَبِّلِ الْعَتَبَةَ وَقَدِّمْ رِجْلَكَ الْيُمْنَىٰ قَبْلَ الْيُسْرَىٰ

towards the sacred shrine with that same state of humbleness which we mentioned previously. In addition, we should avoid any unnecessary actions such as running and the like, and all frivolous talking - especially about the material world. In today's day and age, this would also mean that we should avoid talking on our cellphones, text-messaging, e-mailing, etc. - basically anything which would detract us from our intended goal.

8. Speaking Softly

The individual whom we are visiting does not require us to yell when we address them; there is no need to raise one's voice during the *ziyārah,* or the recitation of any *duʿāʾ* - for they can hear us even if we whisper, or just speak in our heart - therefore, when we approach the shrine and begin to recite the *ziyārah* text, we need to ensure that we keep our voices to a minimum so that we do not disturb others who we are sharing this sacred space with.

Allah ﷻ tells us in the Noble Quran: "O you who believe! Do not raise your voices above the voice of the Prophet, and do not speak out loud to him as you shout to one another, lest your works should fail without your being aware. Indeed, those who lower their voices in the presence of the Messenger of Allah - they are the ones whose hearts Allah has tested for God-consciousness. For them will be forgiveness and a great reward."[17]

---

[17] Quran, Sūrah al-Ḥujurāt (49), Verses 2-3. The Arabic of this is:

9. Glorifying Allah ﷻ

One of the recommended actions before we recite the actual text of the *ziyārah* is that when our eyes fall upon the sacred shrine, we should glorify Allah ﷻ by saying "أَللهُ أَكْبَرُ" *[Allahu Akbar* - Allah is the Greatest] - and then " لَا إِلٰهَ إِلَّا اللهُ وَحْدَهُ لَا شَرِيكَ لَهُ" *[Lā Ilāha Illāllāh Waḥdahu lā Sharīka Lahu* - There is no deity worthy of worship except Allah, (the One) who has no partner]. This reminds us that it is Allah ﷻ who ennobled these great personalities, and that the fact that they worked sincerely in the way of Allah ﷻ to earn His pleasure.

In a lengthy tradition from Imam Muḥammad al-Bāqir ﵇ we read the following: "Allah will write for the one who pronounces the *takbīr* (أَللهُ أَكْبَرُ - *Allahu Akbar)* while in the presence of the Imam, and says "لَا إِلٰهَ إِلَّا اللهُ وَحْدَهُ لَا شَرِيكَ لَهُ" - *Lā Ilāha Illāllāh Waḥdahu lā Sharīka Lahu* - the attainment of His great pleasure, and for whomsoever Allah writes His great pleasure, it will be incumbent upon Allah to place that person, Ibrāhīm, Muḥammad, and all of the previously sent Prophets in the Adobe of Greatness."[18]

﴿يٰأَيُّهَا الَّذِينَ آمَنُواْ لَا تَرْفَعُواْ أَصْوَاتَكُمْ فَوْقَ صَوْتِ النَّبِيِّ وَلَا تَجْهَرُواْ لَهُ بِالْقَوْلِ كَجَهْرِ بَعْضِكُمْ لِبَعْضٍ أَن تَحْبَطَ أَعْمَالُكُمْ وَأَنتُمْ لَا تَشْعُرُونَ. إِنَّ الَّذِينَ يَغُضُّونَ أَصْوَاتَهُمْ عِندَ رَسُولِ اللهِ أُوْلَـٰئِكَ الَّذِينَ امْتَحَنَ اللهُ قُلُوبَهُمْ لِلتَّقْوَىٰ لَهُم مَّغْفِرَةٌ وَأَجْرٌ عَظِيمٌ﴾

[18] Saffār, Abū Jaʿfar Muḥammad al-, *Baṣā'ir al-Darajāt fī Faḍā'il Āle Muḥammad*, Vol. 1, Pg. 312. The Arabic text of this is as follows:

وَمَنْ كَبَّرَ بَيْنَ يَدَيِ الْإِمَامِ وَقَالَ لَا إِلٰهَ إِلَّا اللهُ وَحْدَهُ لَا شَرِيكَ لَهُ كَتَبَ اللهُ لَهُ رِضْوَانَهُ الْأَكْبَرَ وَمَنْ كَتَبَ اللهُ رِضْوَانَهُ الْأَكْبَرَ يَجِبُ أَنْ يَجْمَعَ بَيْنَهُ وَبَيْنَ إِبْرَاهِيمَ وَمُحَمَّدٍ ﷺ وَالْمُرْسَلِينَ فِي دَارِ الْجَلَالِ

10. Approaching the Ḍarīḥ[19] and Kissing it

If it is possible, and without resorting to pushing, shoving, or hurting other people, one should try one's best to walk towards the *ḍarīḥ* and kiss it.

Some believe that if another person is in the same room as the Prophet, Imam, or sanctified individual, then they do not need to try to go and touch or kiss the *ḍarīḥ* - however, they are mistaken.

The custom of the Ahlul Bayt ﷺ tells us that when they used to visit the grave of the Messenger of Allah ﷺ, they would physically touch his grave and pay respect to him as such.

Imam ʿAlī ibn Ḥusayn ﷺ used to stand next to the grave of the Prophet ﷺ, greet the Messenger of Allah ﷺ, and testify that he (the Prophet ﷺ) had conveyed the message of Allah ﷻ. Then he would recite any prayer that came to his mind. Thereafter, he would lean his back on the very delicate green marble that is attached to the grave of the Messenger of Allah ﷺ. While leaning his back and facing the *qiblah*, he would say: "O Allah! I seek refuge with You in all of my affairs, and I have learned my back on the grave of Muḥammad, Your slave and Your Messenger, and I have turned my face towards the *qiblah* that you chose for Muḥammad. O Allah! I find that I do not have the power to attain the good that I desire for myself, nor do I have the power to avert the harm that I fear. O Allah! I find that all the affairs are in Your Hands, and there is no one needier than me. I need the good that You give me. O Allah! I ask you to decree that which is good for me because no one can keep away Your grace. O Allah! I seek

---

[19] A *ḍarīḥ* is the caged enclosure which is over top of the grave.

refuge with You from replacing my name, from changing my body, or from removing Your blessings upon me. O Allah! Adorn me with piety and beautify me with Your blessings. Give me a long and healthy life and sustain me with the ability to thank You for good health."[20]

11. Turning One's Face Towards the True Qiblah

As much as possible, a person should stand such that one's face is towards Mecca, and one is standing either behind or at the head of the one whom they are making the *ziyārah* to; in other words, one should try to ensure that their back is not facing either the *qiblah* in Mecca, or the 'other *qiblah*' (i.e. the focal point) which is the one whom they are visiting.

---

[20] Ibn Qulaway al-Qummī, *Kāmil al-Ziyārāt*, translated by Sayyid Mohsin Ali Hussaini al-Milani. This book can be found online at: www.thaqalayn.net/book/24. The Arabic text of this is as follows:

كَانَ عَلِيُّ بْنُ الْـحُسَيْنِ عليه السلام يَقِفُ عَلَىٰ قَبْرِ النَّبِيِ صلى الله عليه وآله وَيُسَلِّمُ وَيَشْهَدُ لَهُ بِالْبَلَاغِ وَيَدْعُو بِمَا حَضَرَهُ ثُمَّ يُسْنِدُ ظَهْرَهُ إِلىٰ قَبْرِ النَّبِيِّ صلى الله عليه وآله إِلىٰ الْمَرْمَرَةِ الْـخَضْرَآءِ الدَّقِيقَةِ الْعَرْضِ مِمَّا يَلِي الْقَبْرَ وَيَلْتَزِقُ بِالْقَبْرِ وَيُسْنِدُ ظَهْرَهُ إِلىٰ الْقَبْرِ وَيَسْتَقْبِلُ الْقِبْلَةَ وَيَقُولُ: أَللّٰهُمَّ إِلَيْكَ أَلْـجَأْتُ أَمْرِي وَإِلىٰ قَبْرِ مُحَمَّدٍ صلى الله عليه وآله عَبْدِكَ وَرَسُولِكَ أَسْنَدْتُ ظَهْرِي وَالْقِبْلَةَ الَّتِي رَضِيتَ لِمُحَمَّدٍ صلى الله عليه وآله اسْتَقْبَلْتُ. أَللّٰهُمَّ إِنِّي أَصْبَحْتُ لَا أَمْلِكُ لِنَفْسِي خَيْرَ مَا أَرْجُو لَهَا وَلَا أَدْفَعُ عَنْهَا شَرَّ مَا أَحْذَرُ عَلَيْهَا وَأَصْبَحَتِ الْأُمُورُ بِيَدِكَ وَلَا فَقِيرَ أَفْقَرُ مِنِّي إِنِّي لِمَا أَنْزَلْتَ إِلَيَّ مِنْ خَيْرٍ فَقِيرٌ اللَّهُمَّ أَرِدْنِي مِنْكَ بِخَيْرٍ فَلَا رَادَّ لِفَضْلِكَ. أَللّٰهُمَّ إِنِّي أَعُوذُ بِكَ مِنْ أَنْ تُبَدِّلَ اسْمِي أَوْ أَنْ تُغَيِّرَ جِسْمِي أَوْ تُزِيلَ نِعْمَتَكَ عَنِّي. أَللّٰهُمَّ زَيِّنِّي بِالتَّقْوَى وَجَمِّلْنِي بِالنِّعَمِ وَاعْمُرْنِي بِالْعَافِيَةِ وَارْزُقْنِي شُكْرَ الْعَافِيَةِ.

12. Recite the Accepted Ziyārāt

When greeting the noble personalities, indeed, we can use our "own language" and our "own words," and there is nothing wrong with that when we wish to salute them, however, the best way to greet these individuals is through the text of the various *ziyārāt* which the other infallibles have taught us to recite at the graves.

These beautiful words of visitations and different salutations can be found in the recognized and verified books of *Duʿāʾ*'s such as *Mafātīḥ al-Jinān* of the late Shaykh ʿAbbās al-Qummī (which is also available in English and other languages), and other books compiled specifically for the *ziyārāt* of the Ahlul Bayt 🕮.

13. Two Rakʿat Ṣalāt after Ziyārah

One of the established recommendations is to recite a two *rakʿat ṣalāt* after completing the *ziyārah* - keeping in mind that *ṣalāt* is **only** for Allah 🕮, and every act within it [the standing, bowing, prostration, etc.] are all done with the intention of seeking nearness to Allah 🕮. One should also keep in mind that such prayers carry a grand reward with them as one is praying to Allah 🕮 after visiting His most beloved individuals - and as such, these prayers have the power to impact all of those people whom the person prays for, or asks for the rewards to be dedicated to - the infallible, the person performing the *ziyārah*, one's family members, friends, community, etc.

We read in the traditions that one of the supplications to recite after the *ziyārah* of Imam ʿAlī 🕮 is as follows: "O Allah! I have performed these two *rakʿat* as my gift to my master,

Your obedient servant, brother of Your Messenger, Commander of the Faithful, and master of the successors, ʿAlī ibn Abī Ṭālib, Allah's blessings be upon him and his progeny. O Allah! Bless Muḥammad and the progeny of Muḥammad, and accept this from me, and reward me by them with the rewards due to the good doers. O Allah! To You have I prayed, and to You have I bowed down, and to You have I prostrated, and You and only You, there is no partner with You. This is so because praying, bowing down and prostrating can be to none other than You, because You are Allah, there is no god but You. O Allah! Bless Muḥammad and the progeny of Muḥammad and accept my *ziyārah* and grant me my wish by the status of Muḥammad and his pure progeny with You."[21]

14. Supplication after the Ṣalāt

There are special supplications to be recited after the *ṣalāt* is complete, and these have been narrated in the appropriate books of supplications and *ziyārah*. One should not miss out on this opportunity to continue to ask Allah ﷻ for blessings

---

[21] Mashhadī, Muḥammad ibn Jaʿfar al-, *Al-Mazār*, Pg. 150. The Arabic text of this is as follows:

أَللّٰهُمَّ إِنِّي صَلَّيْتُ هَاتَيْنِ الرَّكْعَتَيْنِ هَدِيَّةً مِنِّي إِلىٰ سَيِّدِي وَمَوْلَايَ وَلِيِّكَ وَأَخِي رَسُولِكَ أَمِيرِ الْمُؤْمِنِينَ وَسَيِّدِ الْوَصِيِّينَ عَلِيِّ بْنِ أَبِي طَالِبٍ صَلَوَاتُ اللّٰهِ عَلَيْهِ وَآلِهِ. أَللّٰهُمَّ فَصَلِّ عَلىٰ مُحَمَّدٍ وَآلِ مُحَمَّدٍ وَتَقَبَّلْهَا مِنِّي وَاجْزِنِي عَلىٰ ذٰلِكَ جَزَآءَ الْمُحْسِنِينَ. أَللّٰهُمَّ لَكَ صَلَّيْتُ وَلَكَ رَكَعْتُ وَلَكَ سَجَدْتُ وَحْدَكَ لَا شَرِيكَ لَكَ لِأَنَّهُ لَا تَكُونُ الصَّلَاةُ وَالرُّكُوعُ وَالسُّجُودُ إِلَّا لَكَ لِأَنَّكَ أَنْتَ اللّٰهُ لَا إِلٰهَ إِلَّا أَنْتَ. أَللّٰهُمَّ صَلِّ عَلىٰ مُحَمَّدٍ وَآلِ مُحَمَّدٍ وَتَقَبَّلْ مِنِّي زِيَارَتِي وَأَعْطِنِي سُؤْلِي بِمُحَمَّدٍ وَآلِهِ الطَّاهِرِينَ

while in such a sacred place.

In addition, each of the different *ziyārāt* that we recite have their own special supplication, which is recommended to be recited following the *ṣalāt*, and these can be found in the appropriate books of prayers and supplications.

15. Recitation of the Quran

Once the above acts have been performed, it is advisable for a person to sit near the individual whom one is visiting and recite the Quran and ask Allah ﷻ to dedicate the reward of the recitation towards the one buried in that shrine. Indeed, the reward will be given to the one whose shrine we are visiting, but also to the one who is reciting the Quran. We are told in a *ḥadīth* that: "When the name of the Prophet is mentioned, offer abundant blessings upon him, for whoever blesses the Prophet a single time will receive a thousand blessings from a row of a thousand angels, and nothing which Allah has created will remain without blessing Allah's servant whom Allah and His angels bless. So, anyone who does not desire all of this is ignorant and conceited, and they are clear from Allah, His Messenger, and the Ahlul Bayt."[22]

---

[22] Shaykh Kulaynī, *Al-Kāfī*, Vol. 2, Pg. 492, Ḥadīth 6. The Arabic text of this is as follows:

إِذَا ذُكِرَ النَّبِيُّ ﷺ فَأَكْثِرُوا الصَّلَاةَ عَلَيْهِ فَإِنَّهُ مَنْ صَلَّى عَلَى النَّبِيِّ ﷺ صَلَاةً وَاحِدَةً صَلَّى اللَّهُ عَلَيْهِ أَلْفَ صَلَاةٍ فِي أَلْفِ صَفٍّ مِنَ الْمَلَائِكَةِ وَلَمْ يَبْقَ شَيْءٌ مِمَّا خَلَقَهُ اللَّهُ إِلَّا صَلَّى عَلَى الْعَبْدِ لِصَلَاةِ اللَّهِ عَلَيْهِ وَصَلَاةِ مَلَائِكَتِهِ فَمَنْ لَمْ يَرْغَبْ فِي هٰذَا فَهُوَجَاهِلٌ مَغْرُورٌ قَدْ بَرِئَ اللَّهُ مِنْهُ وَرَسُولُهُ وَأَهْلُ بَيْتِهِ.

16. Presence of the Heart and Heart-Felt Repentance

When we are in these sacred places, we must be sure that everything we do is done with 'presence of the heart' - knowing where we are and why we are there, and once that is realized, then we can also understand that we need to sit back and think of our past transgressions and make a heart - felt repentance to Allah ﷻ. As well, we need to ensure that we ask the one whom we are visiting to pray for forgiveness on our behalf - this being a Quranic mandate - to ask the Prophet ﷺ, and as an extension his noble family members, to pray to Allah ﷻ for the redemption of our soul.

17. Showing Respect to the Shrine and Volunteers

It goes without saying that the entire shrine complex must be respected as this is a house of Allah ﷻ and one of the homes of His final Prophet ﷺ, and as such, just as we respect our own property, we must be extra vigilant to show care and respect to the houses of the Messenger of Allah ﷺ and his noble family ﷺ.

We must also realize that the people who work in the shrine complex do so as volunteers - from the people who take our shoes and safeguard them, to those who direct the traffic flow, to the sweepers and cleaners, to those who serve food - all of them do this simply for the love of Allah ﷻ and the hope of gaining proximity to Him, as He says in the Quran: "...And whoever venerates the symbols of Allah - indeed that arises from the God-consciousness *(taqwā)* of the hearts."[23]

18. Bidding Farewell

It is with heavy hearts when the time comes that we must separate ourselves from the shrines, as we begin to make our way back home - sometimes thousands of kilometers away.

Who knows if we will have the means and ability to make this beautiful journey ever again?

Therefore, before we leave the city, our final stop should not be the bazaar, the gold market, or any other place, but rather the shrine and the special personality buried there. We need to truly bid farewell to them with tears in our eyes, and pray for the opportunity to visit them again, and that our actions are accepted by the All-High, and we can benefit from this visitation.

As an example, when we depart from Abī ʿAbdillāh al-Ḥusayn ﷺ, the supplication to be read for bidding farewell mentions how our visit should make an impact in our daily lives once we leave the sacred shrine: "O Allah! I plead to You, having prayed and saluted [Your Prophet], to bless Muḥammad and the progeny of Muḥammad, such that You do not make this the last time I visit this resting place; but if you deem it as such, O Allah, then I plead You to resurrect me and gather me in his company, and in that of his forefathers and obedient followers; and if You decree that I should remain alive, O Allah, then I plead You to grant me a return to him, then another return after a return, by Your

---

[23] Quran, Sūrah al-Ḥajj (22), Verse 32. The Arabic of this is:

﴿...وَمَن يُعَظِّمْ شَعَآئِرَ اللهِ فَإِنَّهَا مِن تَقْوَى الْقُلُوبِ...﴾

Mercy, O the Most Merciful One. O Allah! Grant me a truthful tongue among Your servants and endear my heart to visit their shrines. O Allah! Bless Muḥammad and the progeny of Muḥammad, and do not let me be distracted from mentioning Your Name by letting the many affairs of life in this world cause me to overlook the wonders of the glory of these shrines, nor should I be tested by the beautiful things of this life's adornments, nor by the reduction of labour which harms my good deeds and the worry of which fills my heart. Grant me, O Allah, to be independent of the evil doers from among Your creations and grant me wisdom through which I can win Your Pleasure, O the Most Merciful One. Peace be upon you, O angels of Allah, O visitors of the gravesite of Abī Abdillāh."[24]

19. Leaving the Shrine

Just as we mentioned in the etiquette of entering the shrine, we need to ensure that we follow similar courtesies as we leave the shrine - meaning that running, talking about the

---

[24] *Kāmil al-Ziyārat*, Pg. 255. The Arabic text of this is as follows:

أَللّٰهُمَّ إِنِّي أَسْأَلُكَ بَعْدَ الصَّلَاةِ وَالتَّسْلِيمِ أَنْ تُصَلِّي عَلَىٰ مُحَمَّدٍ وَآلِ مُحَمَّدٍ وَأَنْ لَا تَجْعَلَهُ آخِرَ الْعَهْدِ مِنْ زِيَارَتِي إِيَّاهُ فَإِنْ جَعَلْتَهُ يَا رَبِّ فَاحْشُرْنِي مَعَهُ وَمَعَ آبَائِهِ وَأَوْلِيَائِهِ وَإِنْ أَبْقَيْتَنِي يَا رَبِّ فَارْزُقْنِي الْعَوْدَ إِلَيْهِ ثُمَّ الْعَوْدَ إِلَيْهِ بَعْدَ الْعَوْدِ بِرَحْمَتِكَ يَا أَرْحَمَ الرَّاحِمِينَ. أَللّٰهُمَّ اجْعَلْ لِي لِسَانَ صِدْقٍ فِي أَوْلِيَائِكَ وَحَبِّبْ إِلَيَّ مَشَاهِدَهُمْ. أَللّٰهُمَّ صَلِّ عَلَىٰ مُحَمَّدٍ وَآلِ مُحَمَّدٍ وَلَا تَشْغَلْنِي عَنْ ذِكْرِكَ بِإِكْثَارٍ عَلَيَّ مِنَ الدُّنْيَا تُلْهِينِي عَجَائِبُ بَهْجَتِهَا وَتَفْتِنُنِي زَهَرَاتُ زِينَتِهَا وَلَا بِإِقْلَالٍ يَضُرُّ بِعَمَلِي كَدُّهُ وَيَمْلَأُ صَدْرِي هَمُّهُ وَأَعْطِنِي ذٰلِكَ غِنًى عَنْ شِرَارِ خَلْقِكَ وَبَلَاغًا أَنَالُ بِهِ رِضَاكَ يَا رَحْمٰنُ وَالسَّلَامُ عَلَيْكُمْ يَا مَلَائِكَةَ اللّٰهِ وَزُوَّارَ قَبْرِ أَبِي عَبْدِ اللّٰهِ.

material world, and other such things must be refrained from as we leave the presence of these noble personalities whom we were visiting.

20. Helping the Needy

As we walk out of the shrine back into the streets, and the everyday hustle and bustle of the world, we need to ensure that if we run into any needy people who are begging for food or money, we do not turn our backs on them.

The one whom we have just visited would never have denied a poor person even a morsel of food, and if we have just completed their *ziyārah*, what better way to show a change in our character than to follow their example and help the less fortunate ones that we encounter.

The Noble Quran mentions the charity of the family of the Prophet ﷺ as follows: "They (are those who) fulfill their vows and fear a Day whose evil will be widespread. And they give food, out of love for Him, to the needy, the orphan, and the prisoner [saying:] 'We only feed you for the sake of Allah. We do not want from you any reward, nor any thanks.'"[25]

Conclusion

Once we have been able to "complete the *ziyārah*" by ensuring that these 20 steps have been adhered to, then we should know and realize for ourselves that all of the actions

---

[25] Quran, Sūrah al-Insān (76), Verses 7-9. The Arabic of this is:

﴿يُوفُونَ بِالنَّذْرِ وَيَخَافُونَ يَوْمًا كَانَ شَرُّهُ مُسْتَطِيرًا. وَيُطْعِمُونَ الطَّعَامَ عَلَىٰ حُبِّهِ مِسْكِينًا وَيَتِيمًا وَأَسِيرًا. إِنَّمَا نُطْعِمُكُمْ لِوَجْهِ اللهِ لَا نُرِيدُ مِنكُمْ جَزَاءً وَلَا شُكُورًا﴾

that we have done - including the actual *ziyārah* - should result in an inner change in our character and nature; and this should be apparent in us at every stage of our lives after this great journey.

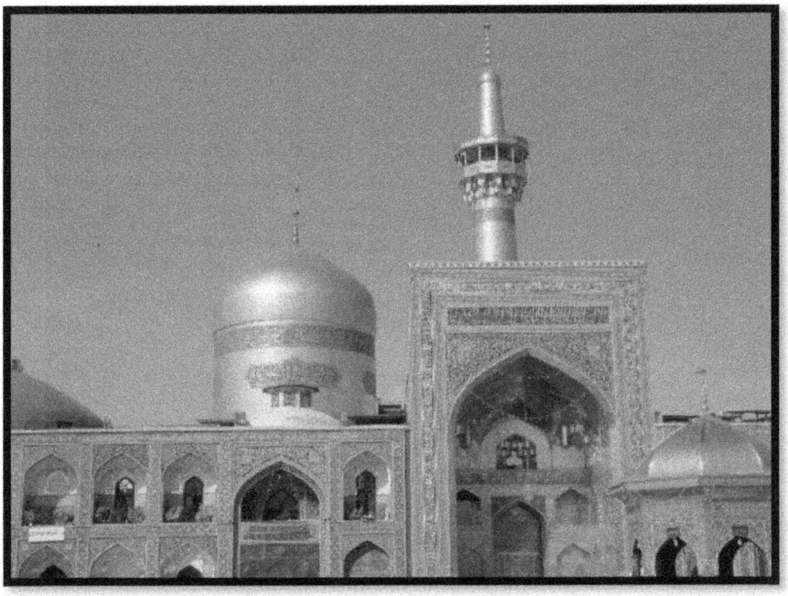

Imam ʿAlī ibn Mūsā al-Riḍā عليهما السلام

Introduction to Imam ʿAlī ibn Mūsā al-Riḍā ﷺ

Out of the 12 Imams of the Ahlul Bayt ﷺ, Imam al-Riḍā ﷺ is the **only** one to be buried "on his own" in the far-off land of Mashhad in Iran.

We know that in Madina (Arabia), the 2nd, 4th, 5th, and 6th Imams ﷺ are buried there; while all of the rest of the Imams ﷺ are buried in Iraq: Kādhimiyyah holds the shrines of the 7th and 9th Imams ﷺ; Samarrah holds the burial spot of the 10th and 11th Imams ﷺ; the 1st Imam ﷺ was laid to rest in Najaf, and the 3rd Imam ﷺ and his companions were buried in Karbalāʾ.

For this reason, the 8th Imam ﷺ is also known as *"gharīb"* or "one who is a stranger in a strange land" - for he was taken by force from the city of the Prophet ﷺ, Madina, to what is today known as Mashhad in the province of Khurāsān in Iran.

Imam ʿAlī ibn Mūsā al-Riḍā ﷺ narrates: "Those who come to my visitation *(ziyārah)* even though my house is far and my grave is distant, will be visited by me on three occasions on the Day of Judgement where I will save them from its terrors. The first occasion is when the books will be distributed to the people of the right and left; the second is on the bridge *(ṣirāṭ)*, and the third is during the [weighing of the actions on the] scale *(mizān)*."[26]

The *Visitation (Ziyārah) of the Seven Traditions (Ḥadīth)* is one of the visitation rites of Imam al-Riḍā ﷺ which has been

---

[26] *Kāmil al-Ziyārāt*, Pg. 444.

narrated in the books, *Ṣaḥīfa Raḍāwiyyah*, compiled by ʿAllāmah Sayyid Murtaḍā Mujtahidī Sīstānī, and *Al-Miṣbāḥ* of Al-Kafʿamī, may Allah shower His mercy upon them both.

The reason why this is known as the *Visitation of the Seven Traditions* is because it contains seven statements: one from Prophet Muḥammad 🌸, one from Imam ʿAlī 🌸, one from Imam Muḥammad al-Bāqir 🌸, one from Imam Jaʿfar al-Ṣādiq 🌸, and the rest from the 8th Imam himself about visiting his shrine.

After performing the *ghusl* for the *ziyārah* (of Imam al-Riḍā 🌸) and following all of the etiquettes for the performance of the *ziyārah* (which we have mentioned in the introduction of this book), we should turn towards the 8th Imam, peace be upon him, and with our back towards the *qiblah*, after making our intention, we should recite his *ziyārah* with the following words.

Ziyārah of Imam ʿAlī ibn Mūsā al-Riḍā (ع)

Translated by Saleem Bhimji

بِسْمِ اللّٰهِ الرَّحْمٰنِ الرَّحِيمِ

In the Name of Allah, the All-Compassionate, the All-Merciful

أَشْهَدُ أَنْ لَا إِلٰهَ إِلَّا اللّٰهُ وَحْدَهُ لَا شَرِيكَ لَهُ،

I bear witness that there is deity except for Allah - the One who has no partners,

وَأَشْهَدُ أَنَّ مُـحَمَّدًا عَبْدُهُ وَرَسُولُهُ،

And I bear witness that Muḥammad is His slave and His Messenger,

وَأَشْهَدُ أَنَّ عَلِيًّا وَلِيُّهُ وَوَصِيُّ رَسُولِهِ.

And I bear witness that indeed ʿAlī is His friend, and the [immediate] successor to His Messenger [Muḥammad (ص)].

أَللّٰهُمَّ صَلِّ عَلٰى مُـحَمَّدٍ وَّآلِ مُـحَمَّدٍ.

O Allah! Send Your prayers upon Muḥammad and the family of Muḥammad.

أَللّٰهُمَّ صَلِّ عَلىٰ الْمَلآئِكَةِ الْمُقَرَّبِينَ،

O Allah! Send Your prayers upon the angels of proximity (to You),

أَللّٰهُمَّ صَلِّ عَلىٰ الْأَنْبِيَآءِ وَالْمُرْسَلِينَ،

O Allah! Send Your prayers upon the [previous] Prophets and the [previous] Messengers,

أَللّٰهُمَّ صَلِّ عَلىٰ الْأَئِـمَّةِ الْمَعْصُومِينَ.

O Allah! Send Your prayers upon the immaculate leaders [the 12 Imams ﷺ].

أَللّٰهُمَّ صَلِّ عَلىٰ مَوْلَانَا وَمُقْتَدَانَا إِمَامِ الْهُدَىٰ،

O Allah! Send Your prayers upon our master, and the one whom we follow, the leader of guidance,

وَالْعُرْوَةِ الْوُثْقَىٰ،

And [the one who is] the firmest handle,

وَحُجَّتِكَ عَلىٰ أَهْلِ الدُّنْيَا،

And [the one who is] Your proof over the people of this world,

أَلَّذِي قَالَ فِي حَقِّهِ سَيِّدُ الْوَرَىٰ وَسَنَدُ الْبَرَايَا:

The one about whom it has been mentioned by the leader of the people, and the support of all creations [Prophet Muḥammad ﷺ]:

سَتُدْفَنُ بَضْعَةٌ مِنِّي بِأَرْضِ خُرَاسَانَ،

"Soon, a part of me [referring to Prophet Muḥammad ﷺ] shall be buried in the land of Khurāsān [Iran],

مَا زَارَهَا مَكْرُوبٌ إِلَّا نَفَّسَ اللّٰهُ كَرْبَهُ،

None who are troubled with grief shall visit [there], except that Allah will alleviate their distress,

وَلَا مُذْنِبٌ إِلَّا غَفَرَ اللّٰهُ ذَنْبَهُ.

And no sinner [will visit there], except that Allah will forgive their sins."

أَللّٰهُمَّ بِشَفَاعَتِهِ الْمَقْبُولَةِ،

O Allah! I ask you by his accepted intercession,

وَدَرَجَتِهِ الرَّفِيعَةِ،

And [I ask you] by his elevated status,

أَنْ تُنَفِّسَ بِهِ كَرْبِي،

That You remove all distress from me,

وَتَغْفِرَ بِهِ ذَنْبِي،

And that You forgive my sin,

وَتُسْمِعَهُ كَلَامِي،

And that You make my words be heard [by him - the 8th Imam ﷺ],

وَتُبَلِّغَهُ سَلَامِي.

And that You convey my regards to him.

أَلسَّلَامُ عَلَيْكَ يَا حُجَّةَ اللّٰهِ،

Peace be upon you, O Proof of Allah,

أَلسَّلَامُ عَلَيْكَ يَا نُورَ اللّٰهِ،

Peace be upon you, O Light of Allah,

أَلسَّلَامُ عَلَيْكَ يَا عَيْبَةَ عِلْمِ اللّٰهِ،

Peace be upon you, O Holder of the Knowledge of Allah,

أَلسَّلَامُ عَلَيْكَ يَا مَعْدِنَ حِكْمَةِ اللّٰهِ،

Peace be upon you, O Repository of the Wisdom of Allah,

أَلسَّلَامُ عَلَيْكَ يَا حَامِلَ كِتَابِ اللّٰهِ،

Peace be upon you, O Custodian of the Book of Allah,

أَلسَّلَامُ عَلَيْكَ يَا حَافِظَ سِرِّ اللّٰهِ.

Peace be upon you, O Guardian of the Secret of Allah.

أَنْتَ الَّذِي قَالَ فِيكَ قَاتِلُ الْكَفَرَةِ،

You [Imam al-Riḍā ﷺ] are the one regarding whom it has been said by the one who fought against the faithless ones,

وَقَامِعُ الْفَجَرَةِ،

And the one who is the repressor of transgression,

عَلِيٌّ أَمِيرُ الْمُؤْمِنِينَ وَوَصِيُّ رَسُولِ رَبِّ الْعَالَمِينَ،

ʿAlī, the Commander of the Faithful, and the successor to the Messenger of the Lord of the Universe,

صَلَوَاتُ اللّٰهِ وَسَلَامُهُ عَلَيْهِ:

May the prayers of Allah and His peace be upon him:

سَيُقْتَلُ رَجُلٌ مِنْ وُلْدِي بِأَرْضِ خُرَاسَانَ بِالسَّمِّ ظُلْمًا،

"Soon, shall a man from my offspring be unjustly killed by poison in the land of Khurāsān (Iran),

إِسْمُهُ إِسْمِي،

His name shall be [the same as] my name [ʿAlī],

وَاسْمُ أَبِيهِ إِسْمُ ابْنِ عِمْرَانَ مُوسىٰ عَلَيْهِ السَّلَامُ.

And the name of his father [shall be the same] name as that of the son of ʿImrān - Mūsā - peace be upon him.

أَلَا فَمَنْ زَارَهُ فِي غُرْبَتِهِ غَفَرَ اللّٰهُ لَهُ ذُنُوبَهُ مَا تَقَدَّمَ مِنْهَا وَمَا تَأَخَّرَ،

So whoever visits him in his loneliness (due to being separated from his family), Allah will forgive that person's sins - those which occurred in the past, and those which will come,

وَلَوْ كَانَتْ مِثْلُ عَدَدِ النُّجُومِ وَقَطَرِ الْأَمْطَارِ وَوَرَقِ الْأَشْجَارِ.

Even if they [those sins] total the number of stars, and the number of raindrops, and the number of leaves on the trees."

مَوْلَايَ مَوْلَايَ، هَا أَنَا ذَا وَاقِفٌ بَيْنَ يَدَيْكَ،

My master [Imam al-Riḍā ﷺ]! My master! Here I am, the one who is standing in your presence,

وَذُنُوبِـي مِثْلُ عَدَدِ النُّجُومِ وَقَطَرِ الْأَمْطَارِ وَوَرَقِ الْأَشْجَارِ،

And my sins are in the number of the stars, and the number of the drops of rain, and the number of leaves on the trees,

وَلَيْسَ لِي وَسِيلَةٌ إِلَى مَـحْوِهَا إِلَّا رِضَاكَ،

And I have no means through which they can be removed except through earning Your pleasure,

مَوْلَايَ مَا أَحْسِبُ فِي صَحِيفَتِي عَمَلًا أَرْجَىٰ عِنْدِي مِنْ زِيَارَتِكَ،

My master! I do not find in my book of deeds, any action, which is greater to me that your visitation *(ziyārah)*,

كَيْفَ وَقَدْ قَالَ فِي حَقِّهَا بَاقِرُ عِلْمِ الْأَوَّلِينَ وَالْآخِرِينَ، صَلَوَاتُ اللهِ عَلَيْهِ:

How can it be when the Splitter of the Knowledge of the First to the Last [Imam Muḥammad ibn ʿAlī al-Bāqir ﵇], prayers of Allah be upon him, has said in his right:

يَـخْرُجُ رَجُلٌ مِنْ وُلْدِي،

"A person shall come from my offspring,

إِسْمُهُ إِسْمُ أَمِيرِ الْمُؤْمِنِينَ،

His name shall be the [same] name as the Commander of the Faithful [ʿAlī ﷺ],

فَيُدْفَنُ بِأَرْضِ خُرَاسَانَ،

He will be buried in the land of Khurāsān [Iran],

مَنْ زَارَهُ عَارِفًا بِحَقِّهِ أَعْطَاهُ اللّٰهُ أَجْرَ مَنْ أَنْفَقَ مِنْ قَبْلِ الْفَتْحِ وَقَاتَلَ.

The one who visits him - fully knowing his rights - will find that Allah shall grant him the reward of a believer who gave in charity before the victory [of Mecca - over the disbelievers] and those who fought."

فَأَتَيْتُكَ زَائِرًا لَكَ،

So therefore, I come to you, paying a visit to you,

عَارِفًا بِحَقِّكَ،

Fully knowing your rights,

عَالِمًا بِأَنَّكَ إِمَامٌ مُفْتَرَضُ الطَّاعَةِ،

Cognizant of the fact that you are the Imam whose obedience is obligatory,

غَرِيبٌ شَهِيدٌ،

[You are one who was] desolate, martyred,

رَاجِيًا بِـمَا قَالَهُ الصَّادِقُ، عَلَيْهِ الصَّلَاةُ وَالسَّلَامُ:

[I am] anticipating that which [Imam] al-Ṣādiq, peace be upon him, said regarding you:

يُقْتَلُ حَفَدَتِي بِأَرْضِ خُرَاسَانَ فِي مَدِينَةٍ يُقَالُ لَـهَا طُوسُ،

"A part of me shall be killed in the land of Khurāsān [Iran] in a city that will be called Ṭūs,

مَنْ زَارَهُ عَارِفًا بِـحَقِّهِ أَخَذْتُهُ بِيَدِي يَوْمَ الْقِيَامَةِ،

I will take that person who visits him - fully knowing his rights - by the hand on the Day of Judgement,

وَأَدْخَلْتُهُ الْـجَنَّةَ،

And will enter that person into Paradise,

وَإِنْ كَانَ مِنْ أَهْلِ الْكَبَآئِرِ.

Even if that person was one who performed the major sins."

قِيلَ لَهُ: مَا عِرْفَانُ حَقِّهِ؟

It was asked of him: "What does it mean to fully know his rights?"

قَالَ: أَلْعِلْمُ بِأَنَّهُ مُفْتَرَضُ الطَّاعَةِ،

He replied: "Knowing that indeed he is the one whose obedience is obligatory,

غَرِيبٌ شَهِيدٌ،

[That he is the] abandoned, a martyr,

مَنْ زَارَهُ عَارِفًا بِحَقِّهِ أَعْطَاهُ اللّٰهُ أَجْرَ سَبْعِينَ شَهِيدًا مِمَّنِ اسْتُشْهِدَ بَيْنَ يَدَيْ رَسُولِ اللّٰهِ، صَلَّى اللّٰهُ عَلَيْهِ وَآلِهِ.

The one who visits him knowing his right will find that Allah will grant him the reward of 70 martyrs who gave their lives in the way of the Messenger of Allah, peace be upon him and his family."

يَا بْنَ رَسُولِ اللّٰهِ،

O son of the Messenger of Allah,

أَبْتَغِي بِزِيَارَتِكَ مِنَ اللّٰهِ تَبَارَكَ وَتَعَالَى غُفْرَانَ ذُنُوبِي وَذُنُوبِ وَالِدَيَّ وَالْمُؤْمِنِينَ وَالْمُؤْمِنَاتِ.

I seek from Allah, the Grand, the Elevated, through [the performance of] your visitation *(ziyārah)*, the forgiveness of my sins, and the sins of my parents and the [sins of the] believing men and the believing women.

وَأَسْأَلُكَ الْإِتْيَانَ الْمَوْعُودَ فِي الْمَوَاطِنِ الثَّلَاثِ:

And I ask you for the promised deliverance in the three stages [in the next life]:

عِنْدَ تَطَايُرِ الْكُتُبِ، وَعِنْدَ الصِّرَاطِ، وَعِنْدَ الْمِيزَانِ.

At the time of the tying of our books of deeds [around our necks]; and at the time of passing over the bridge; and at the time of the weighing of our actions.

وَقُلْتَ وَقَوْلُكَ حَقٌّ:

As you have said, and indeed your words are true:

إِنَّ شَرَّ مَا خَلَقَ اللهُ فِي زَمَانِي يَقْتُلُنِي بِالسَّمِّ،

"Indeed, the worst [person - Maʿmūn al-Rashīd] which Allah has created in my era shall kill me by poison,

ثُمَّ يَدْفُنُنِي فِي دَارِ مَضِيعَةٍ وَبِلَادِ غُرْبَةٍ،

Thereafter, he will bury me in a constrained abode and a barren land,

أَلَا فَمَنْ زَارَنِي فِي غُرْبَتِي كَتَبَ اللهُ عَزَّ وَجَلَّ لَهُ أَجْرَ مِائَةِ أَلْفِ حَاجٍّ وَمُعْتَمِرٍ،

Therefore, [know that] the one who will visit me in my solitude, Allah, the Noble and Grand, will write for them the reward of one hundred thousand accepted *Ḥajj* and *ʿUmrah*,

وَمِائَةِ أَلْفِ مُـجَاهِدٍ،

And [the reward of] one hundred thousand people who struggle in the way (of Allah ﷻ),

وَحُشِرَ فِي زُمْرَتِنَا،

And that person will be raised in our [the Ahlul Bayt's ﷺ] ranks,

وَجُعِلَ فِي الدَّرَجَاتِ الْعُلْـيَ مِنَ الْـجَنَّةِ رَفِيقَنَا،

And that person will be placed in the loftiest levels in Paradise as our friend."

أَلْـحَمْدُ لِلّٰهِ الَّذِي وَفَّقَنِي لِزِيَارَتِكَ فِي الْبُقْعَةِ الَّتِي قُلْتَ فِي حَقِّهَا:

All praise belongs to Allah who has honoured me with the Divine Success *(Tawfīq)* to perform your visitation in a location for which regarding its merits, You have stated:

هِيَ وَاللّٰهِ رَوْضَةٌ مِنْ رِيَاضِ الْـجَنَّةِ،

"This is, I swear by Allah, a garden from among the gardens of Paradise,

مَنْ زَارَنِي فِي تِلْكَ الْبُقْعَةِ كَانَ كَمَنْ زَارَ رَسُولَ اللّٰهِ صَلَّى اللّٰهُ عَلَيْهِ وَآلِهِ،

The one who visits me in such a locality is as the one who visited the Messenger of Allah, peace be upon him and his family,

وَكَتَبَ اللّٰهُ لَهُ ثَوَابَ أَلْفِ حَجَّةٍ مَبْرُورَةٍ،

And Allah will write for such a person the reward of one thousand accepted *Ḥajj*,

وَأَلْفِ عُمْرَةٍ مَقْبُولَةٍ،

And one thousand accepted *ʿUmrah*,

وَكُنْتُ أَنَا وَآبَائِي شُفَعَائَهُ يَوْمَ الْقِيَامَةِ،

And I and my forefathers will intercede for this person on the Day of Judgement."

فَكُنْ شَفِيعِي بِآبَائِكَ الطَّاهِرِينَ وَأَوْلَادِكَ الْمُنْتَجَبِينَ.

So then be my intercessor along with your purified forefathers and your chosen progeny.

مَوْلَايَ، أَنْتَ الَّذِي لَا يَزُورُكَ إِلَّا الْـخَوَاصُّ مِنَ الشِّيعَةِ،

O my master! You are the one whom none visit you except your limited followers (Shīʿas),

فَبِحَقِّكَ وَبِحَقِّ شِيعَتِكَ أَنْ تَشْفَعَنِي،

So then by your right and by the right of your followers (Shīʿas), intercede for me,

وَنَسْأَلُ اللّٰهَ أَنْ يَحْشُرَنِي مَعَ شِيعَتِكَ فِي مُسْتَقَرٍّ مِنَ الرَّحْمَةِ مَعَكُمْ أَهْلَ الْبَيْتِ،

And I ask Allah that He raise me up [on the Day of Judgement] along with your true followers (Shīʿas) in the secure area of mercy with you, the Ahlul Bayt,

مَعَكُمْ مَعَكُمْ لَا مَعَ غَيْرِكُمْ،

I am with you and with those who are with you, and I am not with anyone other than you all,

بَرِئْتُ إِلَى اللّٰهِ مِنْ أَعْدَآئِكُمْ،

I seek immunity with Allah from your enemies,

وَتَقَرَّبْتُ بِاللّٰهِ إِلَيْكُمْ،

And I seek closeness to Allah through you,

إِنِّي مُؤْمِنٌ بِإِيَابِكُمْ،

Indeed, I am a firm believer in your coming back,

مُصَدِّقٌ بِرَجْعَتِكُمْ،

[and] I have a deep conviction in your return [before the end of this world - referring to the *Raj'at*],

مُتَرَقِّبٌ لِدَوْلَتِكُمْ،

Expectant of your kingdom,

عَارِفٌ بِعِظَمِ شَأْنِكُمْ،

Completely aware of the loftiness of your status and ranking,

عَالِمٌ بِضَلَالَةِ مَنْ خَالَفَكُمْ،

Having full knowledge of the misguidance of those people who are against you,

مُوَالٍ لَكُمْ وَلِأَوْلِيَآئِكُمْ،

A sincere friend to you and to your friends,

مُبْغِضٌ لِأَعْدَائِكُمْ،

Having animosity with your enemies,

عَائِذٌ بِكُمْ لَائِذٌ بِقُبُورِكُم.

Taking refuge with you and taking sanctuary in your shrines.

أَللّٰهُمَّ صَلِّ عَلَى مُحَمَّدٍ وَّآلِ مُحَمَّدٍ النَّبِيِّ،

O Allah! Send Your prayers upon Muḥammad and the
family of Muḥammad, the Prophet,

وَالوَصِيِّ وَالْبَتُولِ،

And [send Your prayers] upon Your [Prophet's] successor
['Alī ibn Abī Ṭālib] and al-Batūl [Fāṭima al-Zahrā']

وَالسِّبْطَيْنِ وَالسَّجَّادِ،

and on the two youth [of Paradise - Ḥasan and Ḥusayn],
and al-Sajjād ['Alī ibn al-Ḥusayn],

وَالْبَاقِرِ وَالصَّادِقِ،

and al-Bāqir [Muḥammad ibn 'Alī], and al-Ṣādiq [Ja'far
ibn Muḥammad],

وَالْكَاظِمِ وَالرِّضَا،

and al-Kāẓim [Mūsā ibn Ja'far], and al-Riḍā ['Alī ibn
Mūsā],

وَالتَّقِيِّ وَالنَّقِيِّ،

and al-Taqī [Muḥammad ibn 'Alī], and al-Naqī ['Alī ibn
Muḥammad],

وَالْعَسْكَرِيِّ،

and al-ʿAskarī [Ḥasan ibn ʿAlī ﷺ],

وَالْمَهْدِيِّ صَاحِبِ الزَّمَانِ، صَلَوَاتُكَ عَلَيْهِمْ أَجْمَعِينَ.

and al-Mahdī, Ṣāḥib al-Zamān - may Your prayers be upon all of them.

أَللّٰهُمَّ إِنَّ هٰؤُلَاءِ أَئِمَّتُنَا وَسَادَتُنَا وَقَادَتُنَا وَهُدَاتُنَا وَدُعَاتُنَا.

O Allah! Indeed, these individuals are our Imams, and our masters, and our leaders, and our guides, and our callers (to You).

أَللّٰهُمَّ وَفِّقْنَا لِطَاعَتِهِمْ،

O Allah, enable us to unconditionally obey them,

وَارْزُقْنَا شَفَاعَتَهُمْ،

And give us the good fortune of their intercession,

وَاحْشُرْنَا فِي زُمْرَتِهِمْ،

And raise us up [on the Day of Judgement] in their ranks,

وَاجْعَلْنَا مِنْ خِيَارِ مَوَالِيهِمْ،

And make us from amongst their choicest associates,

بِرَحْـمَتِكَ يَا أَرْحَمَ الرَّاحِـمِينَ،

Through Your Mercy, O the Most Merciful of all those who show mercy,

صَلَّى اللّٰهُ عَلَى مُـحَمَّدٍ وَّآلِهِ الطَّيِّبِينَ الطَّاهِرِينَ الْمَعَصُومِينَ.

Blessings of Allah be upon Muḥammad and his family, the purified, the pure, the immaculate ones.

وَالْـحَمْدُ لِلّٰهِ رَبِّ الْعَالَمِينَ.

And all praise belongs to Allah - Lord of the Worlds.

At this point, one should proceed towards the side of the grave where the head of Imam al-Riḍā ﷺ is, perform a two *rakʿat ṣalāt* for the visitation *(ziyārah),* and then ask Allah ﷻ for one's legitimate desires.

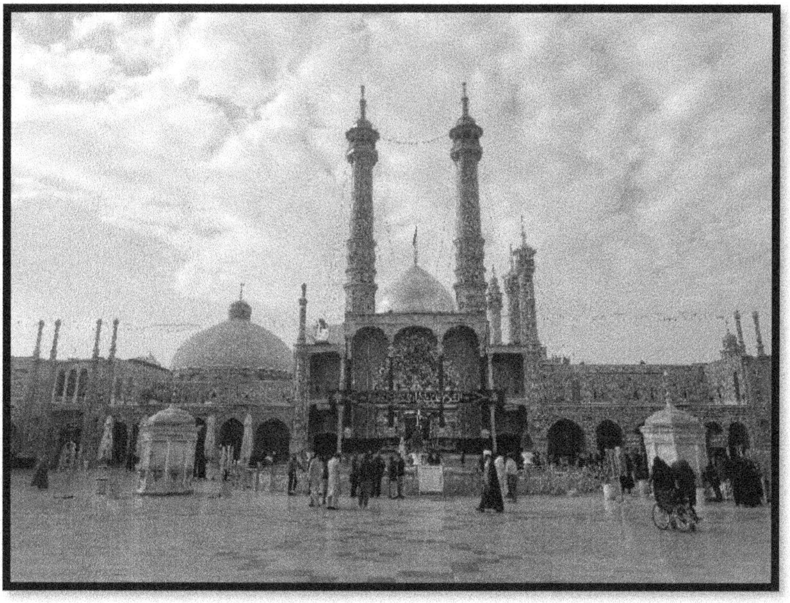

Lady Fāṭima Maʿṣūma bint Mūsā ibn Jaʿfar عليهم السلام

Introduction to Lady Fāṭima Maʿṣūma ﷺ

Lady Fāṭima Maʿṣūma ﷺ - commonly known as Lady Fāṭima Maʿṣūma-e-Qum - was born on the 1st of Dhul Qaʿdah, in the year 173 AH in Madina; and she was the daughter of the 7th successor of Prophet Muḥammad ﷺ, Imam Mūsā al-Kāẓim ﷺ.

There are differing accounts regarding the death of Fāṭima bint Mūsā ibn Jaʿfar. The main opinions on how she died or was killed are as follows.

Living through tumultuous times, such as seeing her beloved brother, Imam ʿAlī ibn Mūsā al-Riḍā ﷺ being taken by force from Madina and eventually having to settle in Mashad, she left Madina to be in the company of her brother.

According to some narrations, she reached the city of Qum in the year 201 AH and saw it draped in black cloth with the masses lamenting. When she enquired as to why they were in such a state of grief, the people of the city, not knowing who she was, told her that their Imam, ʿAlī ibn Mūsā al-Riḍā ﷺ had been killed a few days earlier.

Upon hearing this heart-wrenching news, she collapsed and passed away shortly thereafter - being laid to rest in the city of Qum which was known for its love, honour, and generosity to the Ahlul Bayt ﷺ.

A more widely reported opinion is that Fāṭima al-Maʿṣūma was poisoned. Some accounts state that she was poisoned by a woman after surviving an attack by agents of the caliph in Saveh. It is said that after being poisoned, Fāṭima became ill and asked to be taken to Qum, where she ultimately died.

Today, some 1,200 years later, the city of Qum still enjoys the status of being the gathering place of the true lovers and followers of the Prophet ﷺ and his noble family ﷺ.

The grandfather of Lady Fāṭima Maʿṣūma ﷺ, Imam Jaʿfar al-Ṣādiq ﷺ, said the following about her - around 45 years before her birth even:

تُقْبَضُ فِيهَا إِمْرَاةٌ مِنْ وُلْدِي، إِسْمُهَا فَاطِمَةُ بِنْتِ مُوسَى، وَتَدْخُلُ بِشَفَاعَتِهَا شِيعَتِي الْجَنَّةَ بَأَجْمَعِهِمْ.

"A woman from my descendants will be taken (die) in it (Qum), her name is Fāṭima, daughter of Mūsā, and through her intercession - all my Shīʿas will enter Paradise."

In a *ḥadīth*, Imam al-Jawād ﷺ narrates: "A person who performs the visitation *(ziyārah)* of my aunt (Lady Fāṭima al-Maʿṣūma) in Qum will be rewarded with Paradise."[27]

Buried within the vicinity of her shrine are great scholars, some of which include Grand Āyatullāhs: Sayyid Muḥammad Ḥusayn Burūjerdī, Sayyid Muḥammad Riḍā Gulpāygānī, Shaykh Muḥammad Taqī Behjat, Shaykh ʿAlī Arākī, Shaykh Muḥammad Fāḍil Lankarānī, and many others.

---

[27] *Kāmil al-Ziyārat*, Pg. 478.

Ziyārah of Lady Fāṭima Maʿṣūma ﷺ
Translated by Saleem Bhimji

بِسْمِ اللّٰهِ الرَّحْمٰنِ الرَّحِيمِ

In the Name of Allah, the All-Compassionate, the All-Merciful

One should start by reciting the following *tasbīḥ* (which is like that of Lady Fāṭima al-Zahrā ﷺ - however, with a slight variation):

34 Times	*Allahu Akbar*	أَللّٰهُ أَكْبَرُ
33 Times	*SubḥānAllah*	سُبْحَانَ اللّٰهِ
33 Times	*Alḥamdulillāh*	أَلْحَمْدُ لِلّٰهِ

Her *Ziyārah* is as follows:

أَلسَّلَامُ عَلٰى آدَمَ صِفْوَةِ اللّٰهِ.

Peace be upon Ādam, the Selected One of Allah.

أَلسَّلَامُ عَلٰى نُوحٍ نَبِيِّ اللّٰهِ.

Peace be upon Nūḥ, the Prophet of Allah.

أَلسَّلَامُ عَلٰى إِبْرَاهِيمَ خَلِيلِ اللّٰهِ.

Peace be upon Ibrāhīm, the Friend of Allah.

أَلسَّلَامُ عَلَىٰ مُوسَىٰ كَلِيمِ اللّٰهِ.

Peace be upon Mūsā, the one who Spoke to Allah.

أَلسَّلَامُ عَلَىٰ عِيسَىٰ رُوحِ اللّٰهِ.

Peace be upon ʿIsā, the Spirit of Allah.

أَلسَّلَامُ عَلَيْكَ يَا رَسُولَ اللّٰهِ.

Peace be upon you, O Messenger of Allah.

أَلسَّلَامُ عَلَيْكَ يَا خَيْرَ خَلْقِ اللّٰهِ.

Peace be upon you, O Best of Allah's creations.

أَلسَّلَامُ عَلَيْكَ يَا صَفِيَّ اللّٰهِ.

Peace be upon you, O Selected One of Allah.

أَلسَّلَامُ عَلَيْكَ يَا مُحَمَّدَ بْنِ عَبْدِ اللّٰهِ خَاتَمِ النَّبِيِّينَ.

Peace be upon you, O Muḥammad, son of ʿAbdullāh, the Seal of the Prophets.

أَلسَّلَامُ عَلَيْكَ يَا أَمِيرَ الْمُؤْمِنِينَ عَلِيَّ بْنِ أَبِي طَالِبٍ وَصِيَّ رَسُولِ اللّٰهِ.

Peace be upon you, O Commander of the Faithful, ʿAlī, son of Abī Ṭālib, the Successor of the Messenger of Allah.

أَلسَّلَامُ عَلَيْكِ يَا فَاطِمَةَ سَيِّدَةِ نِسَآءِ الْعَالَمِينَ.

Peace be upon you, O Fāṭima, the Leader of the Women of the Worlds.

أَلسَّلَامُ عَلَيْكُمَا يَا سَبْطَيْ نَبِيِّ الرَّحْمَةِ، وَسَيِّدَيْ شَبَابِ أَهْلِ الْجَنَّةِ.

Peace be upon you, O the two grandsons (Ḥasan and Ḥusayn ﷺ) of the Prophet of Mercy, and the Masters of the Youth of Paradise.

أَلسَّلَامُ عَلَيْكَ يَا عَلِيَّ بْنَ الْحُسَيْنِ سَيِّدَ الْعَابِدِينَ وَقُرَّةَ عَيْنِ النَّاظِرِينَ.

Peace be upon you, O ʿAlī, son of Ḥusayn, the Leader of Worshippers, and Comfort for the Eyes of those who gaze at you.

أَلسَّلَامُ عَلَيْكَ يَا مُحَمَّدَ بْنَ عَلِيٍّ بَاقِرِ الْعِلْمِ بَعْدَ النَّبِيِّ.

Peace be upon you, O Muḥammad, son of ʿAlī, Splitter of the Knowledge after the Messenger.

أَلسَّلَامُ عَلَيْكَ يَا جَعْفَرَ بْنَ مُحَمَّدٍ الصَّادِقَ الْبَارَّ الْأَمِينَ.

Peace be upon you, O Jaʿfar, son of Muḥammad, the Truthful, the Righteous, the Trusted.

أَلسَّلَامُ عَلَيْكَ يَا مُوسىٰ بْنَ جَعْفَرٍ الطَّاهِرَ الطُّهْرَ.

Peace be upon you, O Mūsā, son of Jaʿfar, the Pure, the Purified.

أَلسَّلَامُ عَلَيْكَ يَا عَلِيَّ بْنَ مُوسىٰ الرِّضَا الْـمُرْتَضىٰ.

Peace be upon you, O ʿAlī, son of Mūsā, the Pleased, the Pleasing.

أَلسَّلَامُ عَلَيْكَ يَا مُـحَمَّدَ بْنَ عَلِيٍّ التَّقِيِّ.

Peace be upon you, O Muḥammad, son of ʿAlī, the Pious.

أَلسَّلَامُ عَلَيْكَ يَا عَلِيَّ بْنَ مُـحَمَّدٍ النَّقِيِّ النَّاصِحَ الْأَمِينَ.

Peace be upon you, O ʿAlī, son of Muḥammad, the Pure, the Benevolent, the Trusted.

أَلسَّلَامُ عَلَيْكَ يَا حَسَنَ بْنَ عَلِيٍّ.

Peace be upon Ḥasan, son of ʿAlī.

أَلسَّلَامُ عَلَى الْوَصِيِّ مِنْ بَعْدِهِ.

Peace be upon the successor after him.

أَللّٰهُمَّ صَلِّ عَلٰى نُورِكَ وَسِرَاجِكَ وَوَلِيِّ وَوَلِيِّكَ وَوَصِيِّ وَوَصِيِّكَ وَحُجَّتِكَ عَلٰى خَلْقِكَ.

O Allah, bless Your light and Your torch, the heir of Your vicegerent, the successor of Your appointed successor, and Your guide for Your creations.

أَلسَّلَامُ عَلَيْكِ يَا بِنْتَ رَسُولِ اللّٰهِ.

Peace be upon you, O daughter of the Messenger of Allah.

أَلسَّلَامُ عَلَيْكِ يَا بِنْتَ فَاطِمَةَ وَخَدِيجَةَ.

Peace be upon you, O daughter of Fāṭima and Khadījah.

أَلسَّلَامُ عَلَيْكِ يَا بِنْتَ أَمِيرِ الْمُؤْمِنِينَ.

Peace be upon you, O daughter of the Commander of the Faithful.

أَلسَّلَامُ عَلَيْكِ يَا بِنْتَ الْحَسَنِ وَالْحُسَيْنِ.

Peace be upon you, O daughter of Ḥasan and Ḥusayn.

أَلسَّلَامُ عَلَيْكِ يَا بِنْتَ وَلِيِّ اللّٰهِ.

Peace be upon you, O daughter of the Vicegerent of Allah.

أَلسَّلَامُ عَلَيْكِ يَا أُخْتَ وَلِيِّ اللّٰهِ.

Peace be upon you, O sister of the Vicegerent of Allah.

أَلسَّلَامُ عَلَيْكِ يَا عَمَّةَ وَلِيِّ اللهِ.

Peace be upon you, O aunt of the Vicegerent of Allah.

أَلسَّلَامُ عَلَيْكِ يَا بِنْتَ مُوسىٰ بْنِ جَعْفَرٍ وَرَحْمَةُ اللهِ وَبَرَكَاتُهُ.

Peace be upon you, O daughter of Mūsā, son of Jaʿfar, and may the mercy and blessings of Allah be upon you.

أَلسَّلَامُ عَلَيْكِ عَرَّفَ اللهُ بَيْنَنَا وَبَيْنَكُمْ فِي الْجَنَّةِ،

Peace be upon you - may Allah grant us an acquaintance with you in Heaven,

وَحَشَرَنَا فِي زُمْرَتِكُمْ،

And (may Allah) raise us up [on the Day of Judgement] in your ranks,

وَأَوْرَدَنَا حَوْضَ نَبِيِّكُمْ،

And (may Allah) lead us to your Prophet's fountain,

وَسَقَانَا بِكَأْسِ جَدِّكُمْ مِنْ يَدِ عَلِيِّ ابْنِ أَبِي طَالِبٍ صَلَوَاتُ اللهِ عَلَيْكُمْ.

And quench our thirst with your grandfather's own cup, in the hand of ʿAlī ibn Abī Ṭālib - may Allah's blessings be upon all of you.

أَسْأَلُ اللّٰهَ أَنْ يُرِيَنَا فِيكُمُ السُّرُورَ وَالْفَرَجَ،

I ask Allah to grant us - through you all - happiness and ease,

وَأَنْ يَجْمَعَنَا وَإِيَّاكُمْ فِي زُمْرَةِ جَدِّكُمْ مُحَمَّدٍ صَلَّى اللّٰهُ عَلَيْكُمْ.

And bring us and you into the ranks of your grandfather, Muḥammad - may Allah's blessings be upon all of you.

وَأَنْ لَا يَسْلُبَنَا مَعْرِفَتَكُمْ إِنَّهُ وَلِيٌّ قَدِيرٌ.

And (may He) not deprive us from understanding your status - surely, He is the Guardian, All-Powerful.

أَتَقَرَّبُ إِلَىٰ اللّٰهِ بِحُبِّكُمْ وَالْبَرَاءَةِ مِنْ أَعْدَائِكُمْ،

I seek nearness to Allah through (my) love for you, and through (my) distancing from your enemies,

وَالتَّسْلِيمِ إِلَىٰ اللّٰهِ رَاضِيًا بِهِ غَيْرَ مُنْكِرٍ وَلَا مُسْتَكْبِرٍ،

And I surrender to Allah willingly, neither denying, nor being arrogant,

وَعَلَىٰ يَقِينِ مَا أَتَىٰ بِهِ مُحَمَّدٌ وَبِهِ رَاضٍ.

And I accept with unshaken faith what was brought by Muḥammad and am content with that.

نَطْلُبُ بِذٰلِكَ وَجْهَكَ يَا سَيِّدِي.

We seek Your Providence by this, O my Master.

أَللّٰهُمَّ وَرِضَاكَ وَالدَّارَ الآخِرَةَ.

O my Lord, we seek Your Pleasure in this world and the next world.

يَا فَاطِمَةَ - إِشْفَعِي لِي فِي الْـجَنَّةِ فَإِنَّ لَكِ عِنْدَ اللّٰهِ شَأْنًا مِّنَ الشَّأْنِ.

O Fāṭima! Intercede for me, so that I may enter Heaven, for indeed, you have a great status in the presence of Allah.

أَللّٰهُمَّ إِنِّي أَسْأَلُكَ أَنْ تَـخْتِمَ لِي بِالسَّعَادَةِ فَلَا تَسْلُبْ مِنِّي مَا أَنَا فِيهِ.

O Allah, I ask You to make my destiny good, and not to take away what I have [out of Your Favour] at the present time.

وَلَا حَوْلَ وَلَا قُوَّةَ إِلَّا بِاللّٰهِ الْعَلِيِّ الْعَظِيمِ.

And there is no might or power except that of Allah, the Exalted, the Great.

أَللّٰهُمَّ اسْتَجِبْ لَنَا وَتَقَبَّلْهُ بِكَرَمِكَ وَعِزَّتِكَ وَبِرَحْمَتِكَ وَعَافِيَتِكَ.

O Allah, so then please accept (our supplications) from us through Your Generosity, Your Honour, Your Mercy, and Your Kindness.

وَصَلَّى اللّٰهُ عَلَى مُحَمَّدٍ وَّآلِهِ أَجْمَعِينَ وَسَلَّمَ تَسْلِيمًا يَا أَرْحَمَ الرَّاحِمِينَ.

And may the blessings of Allah be upon Muḥammad and all his Household; and give them abundance and peace. O the Most Merciful of all those who show mercy.

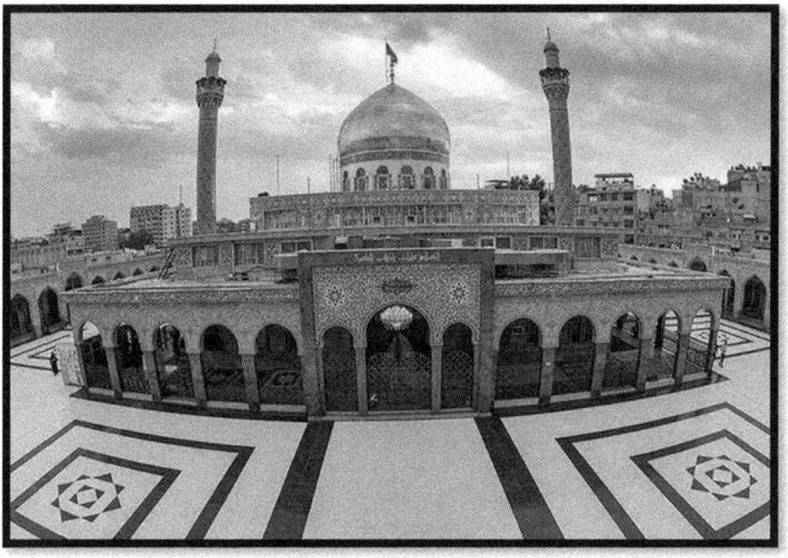

Lady Zaynab bint ʿAlī عليها السلام

Introduction to Lady Zaynab عليها السلام

Lady Zaynab عليها السلام, the daughter of Imam ʿAlī عليه السلام and Lady Fāṭima al-Zahrāʾ عليها السلام, was an exemplary woman of great ability, intelligence, knowledge, insight, courage, and perseverance.

She was born in Madina on the 5th of Jumādī al-Awwal, and lived during the time of Prophet Muḥammad ﷺ, Imam ʿAlī عليه السلام, Lady Fāṭima al-Zahrā عليها السلام, Imam Ḥasan عليه السلام, Imam Ḥusayn عليه السلام, Imam ʿAlī ibn Ḥusayn Zaynul ʿĀbidīn عليه السلام, and Imam Muḥammad ibn ʿAlī al-Bāqir عليه السلام.

Growing up, she experienced a lot of love from the immaculate members of her family. However, at the same time, she also witnessed and directly experienced many tragedies and tribulations during her lifetime:

1. The death of her grandfather - the Messenger of Allah ﷺ.
2. The stealing of the caliphate from her father, Imam ʿAlī عليه السلام.
3. The attack against her mother, Fāṭima al-Zahrāʾ عليها السلام when she was squeezed between the door and the wall.
4. The resulting miscarriage and death of her stillborn brother - Muḥsin عليه السلام.
5. The eventual death of her mother, Fāṭima al-Zahrāʾ عليها السلام, at the tender age of only 18 years.
6. The murder of her beloved father, Imam ʿAlī عليه السلام, while he was in the state of *sajdah* in Masjid al-Kūfa during the blessed month of Ramaḍān.

7. The poisoning and murder of her eldest brother, Imam Ḥasan ibn ʿAlī ‎ﷺ, and his body being assaulted with arrows after his death as it was being taken for burial.
8. The tragic day of ʿĀshūrāʾ when her family, friends, and supporters of the Ahlul Bayt ‎ﷺ were massacred.
9. The merciless attack against her half-brother, Abūl Faḍl ʿAbbās ibn ʿAlī ‎ﷺ, and his martyrdom.
10. The martyrdom of her two young sons - ʿAun and Muḥammad on the plains of Karbalāʾ.
11. The martyrdom of older brother, Imam Ḥusayn ibn ʿAlī ‎ﷺ, who was killed, decapitated, and his body was trampled under the horses of the enemy's army, and then left on the plains of Karbalāʾ without any shroud or burial.
12. Witnessing so many young children who were killed along the way when their caravan was being taken from Karbalāʾ to Kūfa, then Shām. During this painful journey, the women and children were tied in chains and often beaten as well.

Seeing all that she did in her 57 years in this world must have weighed heavily upon her heart.

In addition to all these events, even after the tragic massacre in Karbalāʾ, she continued her struggles to try and awaken the masses to the corrupt leadership at the helm of Islam, and this caused her to be exiled from place to place in many distant lands.

Ultimately, she left this world in the month of Rajab just a few years after the sorrowful events of Karbalāʾ, and like her mother, her exact burial spot is not exactly known.

Although there are numerous reports of where she died and was buried - such as Cairo (Egypt), or in Madina itself -

the overwhelming opinion of the historians is that she died and was laid to rest in Shām (Damascus) in the area now commonly known as *Zaynabiyyah.*

Today, her shrine is a gathering point for lovers of the Prophet ﷺ and his family ﷺ who visit her shrine throughout the year to pay their respects to this heroine of Karbalāʾ and beyond...

Ziyārah of Lady Zaynab bint ʿAlī 🌸
Extracted from Various Sources with Modifications

بِسْمِ اللهِ الرَّحْمٰنِ الرَّحِيمِ

In the Name of Allah, the All-Compassionate, the All-Merciful

أَلسَّلَامُ عَلَيْكِ يَا بِنْتَ سَيِّدِ الْأَنْبِيَآءِ،

Peace be upon you, O daughter of the leader of the Prophets,

أَلسَّلَامُ عَلَيْكِ يَا بِنْتَ صَاحِبِ الْحَوْضِ وَاللِّوَآءِ،

Peace be upon you, O daughter of the owner of the (Heavenly) pond and the flag [of guidance],

أَلسَّلَامُ عَلَيْكِ يَا بِنْتَ مَنْ عُرِجَ بِهِ إِلَى السَّمَآءِ،

Peace be upon you, O daughter of him who was taken to the skies [during the Meʿrāj],

وَوَصَلَ إِلَىٰ مَقَامِ قَابَ قَوْسَيْنِ أَوْ أَدْنَىٰ.

And who reached the position of being [in the proximity of Allah in the amount of] the length of two arrows or even closer.

أَلسَّلَامُ عَلَيْكِ يَا بِنْتَ نَبِيِّ الْهُدَىٰ،

Peace be upon you, O daughter of the Prophet of guidance,

وَسَيِّدِ الوَرَىٰ،

And the master of the upright ones,

وَمُنْقِذِ الْعِبَادِ مِنَ الرَّدَى.

And the saviour of the servants (of Allah ﷻ) from being destroyed.

أَلسَّلَامُ عَلَيْكِ يَا بِنْتَ صَاحِبِ الْـخُلُقِ الْعَظِيمِ،

Peace be upon you, O daughter of the one who conformed (oneself) to sublime morality,

وَالشَّرَفِ الْعَمِيمِ،

And one who enjoyed great honour,

وَالْآيَاتِ وَالذِّكْرِ الْـحَكِيمِ.

And retained the Divine-signs and the wise Remembrance [the Noble Quran].

أَلسَّلَامُ عَلَيْكِ يَا بِنْتَ صَاحِبِ الْمَقَامِ الْـمَحْمُودِ،

Peace be upon you, O daughter of the possessor of the exalted status *[Maqām al-Maḥmūd]*,

وَالْـحَوضِ الْمَوْرُودِ وَاللِّوَآءِ الْمَشْهُودِ.

And the fountain from which people shall drink [on the Day of Judgement], and the flag, which will be witnessed by everyone.

أَلسَّلَامُ عَلَيْكِ يَا بِنْتَ مَنْهَجِ دِينِ الْإِسْلَامِ،

Peace be upon you, O daughter of the [one who is considered as the] path of Islam,

وَصَاحِبِ الْقِبْلَةِ وَالْقُرْآنِ،

And the one given the *Qiblah* [in Mecca] and the Quran,

وَعَلَمِ الصِّدْقِ وَالْـحَقِّ وَالْإِحْسَانِ.

And the flag of honesty, the truth, and benevolence.

أَلسَّلَامُ عَلَيْكِ يَا بِنْتَ صَفْوَةِ الْأَنْبِيَآءِ،

Peace be upon you, O daughter of the chosen one among the Prophets,

وَعَلَمِ الْأَتْقِيَآءِ وَمَشْهُورِ الذِّكْرِ فِي الْأَرْضِ وَالسَّمآءِ،

The example of the pious ones, and the well-known ones, the one who is remembered upon the earth and in the heavens,

وَرَحْمَةُ اللّٰهِ وَبَرَكَاتُهُ.

And may the mercy of Allah and His blessings (be upon you).

أَلسَّلَامُ عَلَيْكِ يَا بِنْتَ خَيْرِ خَلْقِ اللّٰهِ،

Peace be upon you, O daughter of the best of Allah's creation,

وَسَيِّدِ خَلْقِهِ،

And the master of His creatures,

وَأَوَّلِ الْعَدَدِ قَبْلَ إِيْـجَادِ أَرْضِهِ وَسَمَاوَاتِهِ،

And the first created individual before the existence of His earth and His heavens,

وَآخِرِ الْأَبَدِ بَعْدَ فَنَآءِ الدُّنْيَا وَأَهْلِهَا،

And the last of the existent ones (who shall endure) after the extinction of this world and all its beings,

الَّذِي رُوحُهُ نُسْخَةُ الْلاَهُوتِ،

He is the one whose soul reflects the Divine,

وَصُورَتُهُ نُسْخَةُ الْمُلْكِ وَالْمَلَكُوتِ،

And whose appearance reflects the Sovereignty and Kingdom [of Allah],

وَقَلْبُهُ خُزَّانَةُ الْحَيِّ الَّذِي لَا يَمُوتُ،

And whose heart is the treasury of the Eternal, Subsistent One who shall never die,

وَرَحْمَةُ اللهِ وَبَرَكَاتُهُ.

And may the mercy of Allah and His blessings (be upon you).

أَلسَّلَامُ عَلَيْكِ يَا بِنْتَ الْـمُظَلَّلِ بِالغَمَامِ سَيِّدِ الكَوْنَيْنِ وَمَوْلَىٰ الثَّقَلَيْنِ وَشَفِيعِ الْأُمَّةِ يَومَ الْـمَحْشَرِ،

Peace be upon you, O daughter of the one who was shaded by the clouds; is the master of the two worlds; is the chief of the two types of created beings (humanity and *jinn*); and who will be the intercessor of the Muslim nation on the Day of Resurrection,

وَرَحْمَةُ اللهِ وَبَرَكَاتُهُ.

And may the mercy of Allah and His blessings (be upon you).

أَلسَّلَامُ عَلَيْكِ يَا بِنْتَ سَيِّدِ الْأَوْصِيَاءِ.

Peace be upon you, O daughter of the master of the Prophets' successors.

أَلسَّلَامُ عَلَيْكِ يَا بِنْتَ إِمَامِ الْأَتْقِيَآءِ.

Peace be upon you, O daughter of the leader of the God-fearing ones.

أَلسَّلَامُ عَلَيْكِ يَا بِنْتَ رُكْنِ الْأَوْلِيَآءِ.

Peace be upon you, O daughter of the shelter of the friends of Allah.

أَلسَّلَامُ عَلَيْكِ يَا بِنْتَ عِمَادِ الْأَصْفِيَآءِ.

Peace be upon you, O daughter of the support of the chosen ones.

أَلسَّلَامُ عَلَيْكِ يَا بِنْتَ يَعْسُوبِ الدِّينِ.

Peace be upon you, O daughter of the leader of the religion.

أَلسَّلَامُ عَلَيْكِ يَا بِنْتَ أَمِيرِ الْمُؤْمِنِينَ.

Peace be upon you, O daughter of the Commander of the Faithful.

أَلسَّلَامُ عَلَيْكِ يَا بِنْتَ سَيِّدِ الْوَصِيِّينَ.

Peace be upon you, O daughter of the foremost of the Prophets' successors.

أَلسَّلَامُ عَلَيْكِ يَا بِنْتَ قَآئِدِ الْبَرَرَةِ.

Peace be upon you, O daughter of the upright leader.

أَلسَّلَامُ عَلَيْكِ يَا بِنْتَ قَامِعِ الْكَفَرَةِ وَالْفَجَرَةِ.

Peace be upon you, O daughter of the preventer of the infidels and the open transgressors.

أَلسَّلَامُ عَلَيْكِ يَا بِنْتَ وَارِثِ النَّبِيِّينَ.

Peace be upon you, O daughter of the inheritor of the Prophets.

أَلسَّلَامُ عَلَيْكِ يَا بِنْتَ خَلِيفَةِ سَيِّدِ الْمُرْسَلِينَ.

Peace be upon you, O daughter of the successor of the Messengers' chief.

أَلسَّلَامُ عَلَيْكِ يَا بِنْتَ ضِيَآءِ الدِّينِ.

Peace be upon you, O daughter of the illumination of the religion.

أَلسَّلَامُ عَلَيْكِ يَا بِنْتَ النَّبَإِ العَظِيمِ عَلَى الْيَقِينِ.

Peace be upon you, O daughter of the great news (who was) on certainty.

أَلسَّلَامُ عَلَيْكِ يَا بِنْتَ مَنْ حِسَابُ النَّاسِ عَلَيْهِ،

Peace be upon you, O daughter of the one to whom the responsibility of settling the accounts of the people (on the Day of Judgement) will be given,

وَالكَوْثَرُ بَينَ يَدَيْهِ،

And the one between whose hands the Heavenly Pond *(al-Kawthar)* will be put,

وَالنَّصُّ يَومَ الْغَدِيرِ عَلَيْهِ.

And who was intended by the (Prophet's) statement on the Day of *Ghadīr* (the 18th of Dhul Ḥijjah).

وَرَحْمَةُ اللهِ وَبَرَكَاتُهُ.

And may the mercy of Allah and His blessings (be upon you).

أَلسَّلَامُ عَلَيْكِ يَا بِنْتَ مَنْ قَادَ زِمَامَ نَاقَتِهَا جِبرَآئِيلُ،

Peace be upon you, O daughter of the lady whose she-camel was led by (the Archangel) Jibrāʾīl,

وَشَارَكَهَا فِي مُصَابِهَا إِسْرَافِيلُ،

And whose misfortune (of Imam Ḥusayn being killed in Karbalāʾ) was shared by (the Archangel) Isrāʾfīl,

وَغَضِبَ بِسَبَبِهِ الرَّبُّ الْجَلِيلُ،

And due to whose anger, the All-Exalted Lord was angry,

وَبَكَى لِمُصَابِهَا إِبْرَاهِيمُ الْخَلِيلُ وَنُوحٌ وَمُوسَىٰ الْكَلِيمُ فِي كَرْبَلَآءَ.

And for those misfortunes in Karbalāʾ, (the Prophets) Ibrāhīm - the Friend of Allah, and Nūḥ, and Mūsā - the one Spoken to by Allah, (all) wept.

أَلسَّلَامُ عَلَيْكِ يَا بِنْتَ الْبُدُورِ السَّوَاطِعِ.

Peace be upon you, O daughter of the radiant moons.

أَلسَّلَامُ عَلَيْكِ يَا بِنْتَ الشُّمُوسِ الطَّوَالِعِ،

Peace be upon you, O daughter of the brilliant suns,

وَرَحْمَةُ اللهِ وَبَرَكَاتُهُ.

And may the mercy of Allah and His blessings (be upon you).

أَلسَّلَامُ عَلَيْكِ يَا بِنْتَ زَمْزَمَ وَالصَّفَا.

Peace be upon you, O daughter of [the well of] Zamzam, and [the mountain of] al-Ṣafā (two of the landmarks of Mecca).

أَلسَّلَامُ عَلَيْكِ يَا بِنْتَ مَكَّةَ وَمِنىٰ.

Peace be upon you, O daughter of Mecca and Minā.

أَلسَّلَامُ عَلَيْكِ يَا بِنْتَ مَنْ حُمِلَ عَلَى الْبُرَاقِ فِي الْهَوَآءِ.

Peace be upon you, O daughter of the one who was carried by *al-Burāq* to the heavens.

أَلسَّلَامُ عَلَيْكِ يَا بِنْتَ مَنْ حَمَلَ الزَّكَاةَ بِأَطْرَافِ الرِّدَآءِ وَبَذَلَهَا عَلَى الْفُقَرَآءِ.

Peace be upon you, O daughter of the one who carried the *zakāt* in a robe to give it to the indigent ones.

أَلسَّلَامُ عَلَيْكِ يَا بِنْتَ مَنْ أُسْرِيَ بِهِ مِنَ الْمَسْجِدِ الْحَرَامِ إِلَى الْمَسْجِدِ الْأَقْصَىٰ.

Peace be upon you, O daughter of the one who was taken by night from the Inviolable Masjid *[Masjid al-Ḥarām]* to the Farthest Masjid *[Masjid al-Aqsā]*.

أَلسَّلَامُ عَلَيْكِ يَا بِنْتَ مَنْ ضَرَبَ بِالسَّيْفَيْنِ.

Peace be upon you, O daughter of the one who fought with two swords.

أَلسَّلَامُ عَلَيْكِ يَا بِنْتَ مَنْ صَلَّى الْقِبْلَتَيْنِ.

Peace be upon you, O daughter of the one who offered prayers in the two directions of prayer [Jerusalem and Mecca].

أَلسَّلَامُ عَلَيْكِ يَا بِنْتَ مُحَمَّدٍ الْمُصْطَفَىٰ.

Peace be upon you, O daughter of Muḥammad al-Muṣṭafā.

أَلسَّلَامُ عَلَيْكِ يَا بِنْتَ عَلِيٍّ الْمُرْتَضَىٰ.

Peace be upon you, O daughter of ʿAlī al-Murtaḍā.

أَلسَّلَامُ عَلَيْكِ يَا بِنْتَ فَاطِمَةَ الزَّهْرَآءِ.

Peace be upon you, O daughter of Fāṭima al-Zahrāʾ.

أَلسَّلَامُ عَلَيْكِ يَا بِنْتَ خَدِيجَةَ الْكُبْرَىٰ.

Peace be upon you, O daughter of Khadījah al-Kubrā.

أَلسَّلَامُ عَلَيْكِ وَعَلَى جَدِّكِ مُحَمَّدٍ الْمُخْتَارِ.

Peace be upon you and upon your grandfather, Muḥammad al-Mukhtār.

أَلسَّلَامُ عَلَيْكِ وعَلى أَبِيكِ حَيْدَرِ الكَرَّارِ.

Peace be upon you and upon your father, Ḥaydar al-Karrār.

أَلسَّلَامُ عَلَيْكِ وَعَلى السَّادَاتِ الْأَطْهَارِ الْأَخْيَارِ، وَهُمْ حُجَجُ اللّٰهِ عَلى الْأَقْطَارِ وَسَادَاتِ الْأَرْضِ والسَّمَآءِ الَّذِينَ حُبُّهُم فَرَضٌ عَلى أَعْنَاقِ كُلِّ الْـخَلَائِقِ.

Peace be upon you and upon the pure, choice masters who are the Proofs of Allah on the lands, the chiefs of the earth and the heavens, and love for whom is a prescription that is incumbent upon all the creatures.

أَلسَّلَامُ عَلَيْكِ يَا بِنْتَ وَلِيِّ اللّٰهِ الْمُعَظَّمِ.

Peace be upon you, O daughter of the glorified one who has been vested with the authority of Allah (over His creations).

أَلسَّلَامُ عَلَيْكِ يَا عَمَّةَ وَلِيِّ اللّٰهِ الْمُكَرَّمِ.

Peace be upon you, O aunt of the dignified one who has been vested with the authority of Allah (over His creations).

أَلسَّلَامُ عَلَيْكِ يَا أُمَّ الْمَصَآئِبِ يَا زَيْنَبُ.

Peace be upon you, O mother of trials, O Zaynab.

وَرَحْمَةُ اللهِ وَبَرَكَاتُهُ.

And may the mercy of Allah and His blessings (be upon you).

أَلسَّلَامُ عَلَيْكِ أَيَّتُهَا الْفَاضِلَةُ الرَّشِيدَةُ.

Peace be upon you, O the virtuous, the guided one.

أَلسَّلَامُ عَلَيْكِ أَيَّتُهَا الْكَامِلَةُ الْعَالِـمَةُ الْعَامِلَةُ.

Peace be upon you, O the perfect, the knowledgeable, the one who acted according to her knowledge (of the religion).

أَلسَّلَامُ عَلَيْكِ أَيَّتُهَا الْكَرِيـمَةُ النَّبِيلَةُ.

Peace be upon you, O the noble, the gentle woman.

أَلسَّلَامُ عَلَيْكِ أَيَّتُهَا التَّقِيَّةُ النَّقِيَّةُ.

Peace be upon you, O the pious, the devout one.

أَلسَّلَامُ عَلَيْكِ يَا مَنْ ظَهَرَتْ مَـحَـبَّتُهَا لِلْحُسَيْنِ الْمَظْلُومِ فِي مَوَارِدَ عَدِيدَةٍ.

Peace be upon you, O the one who showed her love for Ḥusayn - the oppressed one - in numerous instances.

وَتَـحْمِلُ الْمَصَآئِبَ الْـمُحْرِقَةِ لِلْقُلُوبِ مَعَ تَـحَـمُّلَاتٍ شَدِيدَةٍ.

And bore, with great forbearance, the difficulties which burn the hearts.

أَلسَّلَامُ عَلَيْكِ يَا مَنْ حَفَظَتِ الْإِمَامَ فِي يَومِ عَاشُورَآءَ فِي الْقَتْلىٰ،

Peace be upon you, O the one who guarded the Imam on the Day of ʿĀshūrāʾ when he was being killed,

وَبَذَلَتْ نَفْسَهَا فِي نَـجَاةِ زَيْنِ الْعَابِدِينَ فِي مَـجْلِسِ أَشْقىٰ الْأَشْقِيَآءِ،

And sacrificed her soul for the salvation of Zaynul ʿĀbidīn at the gathering of the most wretched one (ʿUbaydullāh ibn Ziyād),

وَنَطَقَتْ كَنُطْقِ عَلِيٍّ عَلَيْهِ السَّلَامُ فِي سِكَكِ الْكُوفَةِ وَحَوْلَهَا كَثِيرٌ مِنَ الْأَعْدَآءِ.

And addressed a gathering and delivered a speech just like (Imam) ʿAlī, peace be upon him, did in the streets of Kūfa, despite the presence of several enemies.

أَلسَّلَامُ عَلَيْكِ يا مَنْ نَطَحَتْ جَبِينَهَا بِـمُقَدَّمِ الْمَحْمِلِ إِذْ رَأَتْ رَأْسَ سَيِّدِ الشُّهَدَآءِ،

Peace be upon you, O the one who thrust her forehead with the front part of the wooden saddle when she saw the severed head of the Chief of the Martyrs (Imam Ḥusayn ﷺ),

وَيَـخْرُجُ الدَّمُ مِنْ تَـحْتِ قِنَاعِهَا وَمِنْ مَـحْمِلِهَا بِـحَيْثُ يَرىٰ مِنْ حَوْلِـهَا مِنَ الْأَعْدَآءِ.

And caused blood to flow from beneath her veil and from the saddle such that even the enemies around her saw it.

أَلسَّلَامُ عَلَيْكِ يَا تَالِـيَ الْمَعْصُومِ.

Peace be upon you, O follower of the Immaculate [Imam].

أَلسَّلَامُ عَلَيْكِ يَا مُمْتَحَنَةً فِي تَـحَمُّلَاتِ الْمَصَائِبِ كَالْـحُسَيْنِ الْمَظْلُومِ.

Peace be upon you, O the one who was tested through patience during misfortunes, like that of Ḥusayn, the oppressed one.

وَرَحْمَةُ اللهِ وَبَرَكَاتُهُ.

And may the mercy of Allah and His blessings (be upon you).

أَلسَّلَامُ عَلَيْكِ أَيَّتُهَا الْبَعِيدَةُ عَنِ الْأَوْطَانِ.

Peace be upon you, O the one who is far away from your home.

أَلسَّلَامُ عَلَيْكِ أَيَّتُهَا الْأَسِيرَةُ فِي الْبُلْدَانِ.

Peace be upon you, O the one who was marched as a captive through the cities.

أَلسَّلَامُ عَلَيْكِ أَيَّتُهَا الْمُتَحَيِّرَةُ فِي خَرَابَةِ الشَّامِ.

Peace be upon you, O the one who was bewildered [while brought into] that ruined place in Shām (Damascus).

أَلسَّلَامُ عَلَيْكِ أَيَّتُهَا الْـمُتَحَيِّرَةُ فِي وُقُوفِكِ عَلٰى جَسَدِ سَيِّدِ الشُّهَدَآءِ وَخَاطَبْتِ جَدَّكِ رَسُولَ اللّٰهِ صَلَّى اللّٰهُ عَلَيْهِ وَآلِهِ بِهٰذَا النِّدَآءِ:

Peace be upon you, O the one who was in a state of bewilderment as you stood by the (severed) body of the Chief of the Martyrs as you called out to you grandfather, the Messenger of Allah, prayers of Allah be upon him and his family, saying:

صَلَّى عَلَيْكَ مَلآئِكَةُ السَّمَآءِ!

"[O Muḥammad!] May the heavenly angels bless you!

هٰذَا حُسَيْنٌ بِالعَرَآءِ مَسْلُوبُ الْعِمَامَةِ وَالرِّدَآءِ!

This is Ḥusayn under the open sky! His turban and his clothes have been stripped [off his body]!

مُقَطَّعُ الْأَعْضَآءِ!

His limbs have been severed [from his body]!

وَبَنَاتُكَ سَبَايَا!

And your daughters have been taken as prisoners!

وَإِلَىٰ اللهِ الْمُشْتَكَىٰ.

And [we] only complain [about this] to Allah."

وَقَالَتْ: يَا مُحَمَّدُ! هٰذَا حُسَيْنٌ تَسْفَى عَلَيْهِ رِيحُ الصَّبَا.

And she also said: "O Muḥammad! This is Ḥusayn! Winds are blowing over his body.

مَجْذُوذُ الرَّأْسِ مِنَ القَفَا،

His head is cut off from the back,

قَتِيلُ أَوْلَادُ الْبَغَا.

He is being murdered by the illegitimately born ones.

وَاحُزْنَاهُ عَلَيْكَ يَا أَبَا عَبْدِ اللّٰهِ.

O, my grief for you, O Abā ʿAbdillāh.

أَلسَّلَامُ عَلٰى مَنْ تَهَيَّجَ قَلْبُهَا لِلْحُسَيْنِ الْمَظْلُومِ الْعُرْيَانِ الْمَطْرُوحِ عَلٰى الثَّرٰى.

Peace be upon the one whose heart cried out for Ḥusayn; the oppressed, the unclothed, and the one thrown onto the barren ground."

وَقَالَتْ بِصَوتٍ حَزِينٍ:

And she said in a moving voice:

بِأَبِي مِنْ نَفْسِي لَهُ الْفِدَآءُ.

"May my father be sacrificed for the one for whom I sacrifice my soul.

بِأَبِي الْمَهمُومُ حَتّٰى قَضٰى.

May my father be sacrificed for the one who was sorrowful until he passed away.

بِأَبِي الْعَطْشَانِ حَتّٰى مَضٰى.

May my father be sacrificed for the one who had been thirsty (until he departed from this world).

بِأَبِي مَنْ شَيْبَتُهُ تَقْطُرُ بِالدِّمَاءِ.

May my father be sacrificed for the one whose grey beard was dripping in blood."

أَلسَّلَامُ عَلٰى مَنْ بَكَتْ عَلٰى جَسَدِ أَخِيهَا بَيْنَ الْقَتْلٰى حَتّٰى بَكٰى لِبُكَـآئِهَا كُلُّ عَدُوٍّ وَصَدِيقٍ.

Peace be upon the one who wept so severely over the (severed) body of her brother among the ones who had been killed such that everyone - whether enemy or friend - wept with her.

وَرَأَى النَّاسُ دُمُوعَ الْـخَيلِ تَنْحَدِرُ عَلٰى حَوَافِرِهَا عَلٰى التَّحْقِيقِ.

And moreover, people, as it is proved by authenticated narrations, even saw the horses shed tears which fell onto their hoofs.

أَلسَّلَامُ عَلٰى مَنْ تَكَفَّلَتْ وَجْمَعَتْ فِي عَصْرِ عَاشُورَآءٍ بَنَاتِ رَسُولِ اللّٰهِ وَأَطْفَالِ الْـحُسَينِ وَقَامَتْ لَهَا الْقِيَامَةُ فِي شَهَادَةِ الطِّفْلَينِ الغَرِيبَيْنِ الْمَظْلُومَينِ.

Peace be upon the one who took the responsibility of gathering and guarding the daughters of the Messenger of Allah, and the children of Ḥusayn on the afternoon (of the Day of) ʿĀshūrāʾ, and [it was as if] the (Day of) Judgement came when the two young, oppressed children were martyred.

أَلسَّلَامُ عَلٰى مَنْ لَمْ تَـنَمْ عَيْنُهَا لِأَجْلِ حِرَاسَةِ آلِ رَسُولِ اللّٰهِ فِي طَفِّ نَيْنَوىٰ.

Peace be upon the one whose eyes did not sleep to guard the family of the Messenger of Allah at Ṭaff in Naynawāh (Karbalāʾ).

وَصَارَتْ أَسِيرَةً ذَلِيلَةً بِيَدِ الْأَعْدَآءِ.

And they were taken captive and demeaned at the hands of the enemies.

أَلسَّلَامُ عَلٰى مَنْ رَكِبَتْ بَعِيرًا بِغَيرِ وَطَآءٍ وَنَادَتْ أَخِيهَا أَبَا الْفَضْلِ بِهٰذَا النِّدَآءِ:

Peace be upon the one who had to ride a saddleless camel, then she called on her [now martyred] brother Abūl Faḍl (ʿAbbās), saying:

أَخِي أَبَا الْفَضْلِ، أَنْتَ الَّذِي أَرْكَبْتَنِي إِذْ أَرَدْتُ الْـخُرُوجَ مِنَ الْمَدِينَةِ.

"O my brother, Abūl Faḍl! It was you who helped me to mount the camel when I left Madina."

أَلسَّلَامُ عَلَى مَنْ خَطَبَتْ فِي مَيْدَانِ الْكُوفَةِ بِخُطْبَةٍ نَافِعَةٍ حَتّٰى سَكَنَتِ الْأَصْوَاتُ مِنْ كُلِّ نَاحِيَةٍ.

Peace be upon the one who delivered a remarkably expressive speech in the downtown of Kūfa such that she made all the voices (of even the animals) keep silent (as they listened to her with utter astonishment).

أَلسَّلَامُ عَلَى مَنِ احْتَجَّتْ فِي مَجْلِسِ ابْنِ زِيَادٍ بِاحتِجَاجَاتٍ وَاضِحَةٍ وَقَالَتْ فِي جَوَابِهِ بِبَيِّنَاتٍ صَادِقَةٍ، إِذْ قَالَ ابْنُ زِيَادٍ لِزَيْنَبَ سَلَامُ اللّٰهِ عَلَيْهَا:

Peace be upon the one who replied with clear-cut arguments in the gathering of (ʿUbaydullāh) Ibn Ziyād when she said, in a truthful response to Ibn Ziyād's question to Zaynab, prayers of Allah be upon her:

كَيفَ رَأَيْتِ صُنْعَ اللّٰهِ بِأَخِيكِ الْحُسَينِ؟ قَالَتْ: مَا رَأَيْتُ إِلَّا جَمِيلًا!

"How do you see that which Allah did to your brother?" She replied: "I see nothing except beauty!"

أَلسَّلَامُ عَلَيْكِ يَا أَسِيرَةً بِأَيْدِي الْأَعْدَآءِ فِي الْفَلَوَاتِ وَرَأَيْتِ أَهْلَ الشَّامِ فِي حَالَةِ الْعَيشِ والسُّرُورِ وَنَشْرِ الرَّايَاتِ.

Peace be upon you, O who had to be imprisoned at the hands of the enemies under an open sky, and had to see the people of Shām [Damascus] celebrate (the martyrdom of your brother) with pleasure, joy, and raised flags.

أَلسَّلَامُ عَلَىٰ مَنْ شُدَّ الْـحَبْلُ عَلى عَضُدِهَا وَعُنُقِ الْإِمَامِ زَينِ الْعَابِدِينَ وَأَدخَلُوهَا مَعَ سِتَّةَ عَشَرَ نَفَرٍ مِنْ آلِ رَسُولِ اللّٰهِ وَهُمْ كَالْأُسَرَآءِ مُقَرَّنِينَ بِالْـحَدِيدِ مَظْلُومِينَ.

Peace be upon the one who was tied with a rope around the arm, which was linked to the neck of Imam Zaynul ʿĀbidīn, and she - along with sixteen people from the family of the Messenger of Allah - were forced to enter (the gathering of Yazīd) while they were all enchained with iron fetters, oppressed.

وَقَالَ عَلِيُّ بْنُ الْـحُسَينِ عَلَيْهِ السَّلَامُ لِيَزِيدَ: يَا يَزِيدُ مَا ظَنُّكَ بِرَسُولِ اللّٰهِ صَلَّى اللّٰهُ عَلَيْهِ وَآلِهِ لَو رَآنَا عَلىٰ هٰذِهِ الْـحَالَةِ؟

Meanwhile, ʿAlī ibn Ḥusayn (Imam Zaynul ʿĀbidīn), peace be upon him, said to Yazīd: "O Yazīd! What if the Messenger of Allah, peace be upon him and his family, was to see us in such a state? What would his impression be?"

ثُمَّ قَالَتْ أُمُّ الْمَصَآئِبِ زَيْنَبُ لَهُ:

Then Zaynab, the Mother of Misfortunes, said to him [to Yazīd after he had uttered some lines of poetry]:

قَآئِلًا لَأَهَلُّوا وَاسْتَهَلُّوا فَرَحًا.

"Rejoice, raise your voice in joy."

ثُمَّ قَالُوا يَا يَزِيدُ لَا تُشَلْ، مُنْتَحِيًا عَلَىٰ ثَنَايَا أَبِي عَبْدِ اللّٰهِ، سَيِّدِ شَبَابِ أَهْلِ الْـجَنَّةِ تَنْكُتُهَا بِـمَخْصَرَتِكَ؟

Then they (the enemies) said: "O Yazīd, may you not be paralyzed!" as he hit the lips of Abī ʿAbdillāh, the Master of the Youths of Paradise, with a stick.

ثُمَّ قَالَتْ: وَلَئِنْ جَرَّتْ عَلَيَّ الدَّوَاهِي مُـخَاطَبَتَكَ، فَإِنِّي لَأَسْتَصْغِرُ قَدْرَكَ وَأَسْتَعْظِمُ تَقْرِيعَكَ وَأَسْتَكْثِرُ تَوْبِيخَكَ، لٰكِنَّ الْعُيُونَ عَبْرَىٰ وَالصُّدُورَ حَرّٰى. أَلَا فَالعَجَبُ كُلُّ الْعَجَبِ مِنْ إِقْدَامِكَ لِقَتْلِ حِزْبِ اللّٰهِ النُّجَبَآءِ بِـحِزْبِ الشَّيْطَانِ الطُّلَقَآءِ!

Then she said: "Although calamities have forced me to speak to you, I see you trivial in my eyes, and find your verbal attacks great, and I regard your rebuke too much to bear, but the eyes are tearful, and the chests are filled with sorrow. What is even stranger is that the honoured Party of Allah is being killed by the Party of Satan - the 'freed ones!'

وَلَئِنِ اتَّخَذْتَنَا مَغْنَمًا لَتَجِدَنَّا وَشِيكًا مَغْرَمًا حِينَ لَا تَجِدُ إِلَّا مَا قَدَّمَتْ يَدَاكَ، ﴿وَمَا رَبُّكَ بِظَلَّامٍ لِلْعَبِيدِ﴾ فَإِلَىٰ اللّٰهِ الْمُشْتَكَى وَعَلَيْهِ الْمُعَوَّلُ فِي الشِّدَّةِ والرَّخَاءِ.

If you regard us as your plundered war-treasure, then you shall soon find us as your liability - when you will see the consequences of what you have done: 'And your Lord is never unjust to His servants.'[28] To Allah do I complain, and upon Him do I rely in times of difficulty, as well as in ease.

فَكِدْ كَيْدَكَ وَاسْعَ سَعْيَكَ وَنَاصِبْ جُهْدَكَ!

So, scheme whatever you wish to scheme, and carry out your plots, and intensify your efforts!

فَوَ اللّٰهِ لَا تَمْحُوْ ذِكْرِنَا وَلَا تُمِيتُ وَحْيَنَا وَلَا تُدْرِكُ أَمَدَنَا وَلَا تَرْحَضُ عَنْكَ عَارَهَا.

For by Allah, I swear that you shall never be able to obliterate our mention, nor will you ever be able to kill our revelation [that was revealed to us - Islam and the Quran], nor will you ever (be able to) reach to our exalted position, nor will your shame ever be washed away.

---

[28] Quran, Sūrah Fuṣṣilat (41), Verse 46.

وَهَلْ رَأْيُكَ إِلَّا فَنَدٌ، وَأَيَّامُكَ إِلَّا عَدَدٌ، وَجَمْعُكَ إِلَّا بَدَدٌ،
يَا يَزِيدُ أَمَّا سَمِعْتَ قَوْلَ اللهِ تَعَالَىٰ: ﴿وَلَا تَحْسَبَنَّ الَّذِينَ
قُتِلُوا فِي سَبِيلِ اللهِ أَمْوَاتًا بَلْ أَحْيَاءٌ عِنْدَ رَبِّهِمْ يُرْزَقُونَ﴾

Your view will be proven futile, your days are limited in number, and your wealth will be wasted. O Yazīd! Have you not heard Allah, the Almighty say: 'Do not reckon those who are killed in the way of Allah to be dead, rather, they are alive with their Lord being sustained.'[29]

وَحَسْبُكَ بِاللهِ حَاكِمًا وَبِمُحَمَّدٍ صَلَّى اللهُ عَلَيْهِ وَآلِهِ
خَصْمًا وَبِجِبْرِيلَ عَدُوًّا

And Allah is sufficient for you as a judge; and Muḥammad, prayers of Allah be upon him and his family, will argue against you, and Jibrāʾīl will be your enemy."

ثُمَّ قَالَتْ: أَلْحَمْدُ لِلّهِ الَّذِي خَتَمَ لِأَوَّلِنَا بِالسَّعَادَةِ
وَالْمَغْفِرَةِ وَلِآخِرِنَا بِالشَّهَادَةِ وَالرَّحْمَةِ، إِنَّهُ رَحِيمٌ وَدُودٌ،
وَهُوَ حَسْبُنَا وَنِعْمَ الوَكِيلُ.

Then she said: "Praise be to Allah - the one who took away the first of us with prosperity and forgiveness, and the last one of us with martyrdom and mercy; for He is the All-

[29] Quran, Sūrah Āle ʿImrān (3), Verse 169.

Merciful, All-Kind; and He is Sufficient for us, and the Best of the Protectors."

وَصَلَّى اللّٰهُ عَلٰى مُحَمَّدٍ وَّأَهْلِ بَيْتِهِ الطَّيِّبِينَ الطَّاهِرِينَ.

And may Allah bless Muḥammad and his family, the pure, the immaculate.

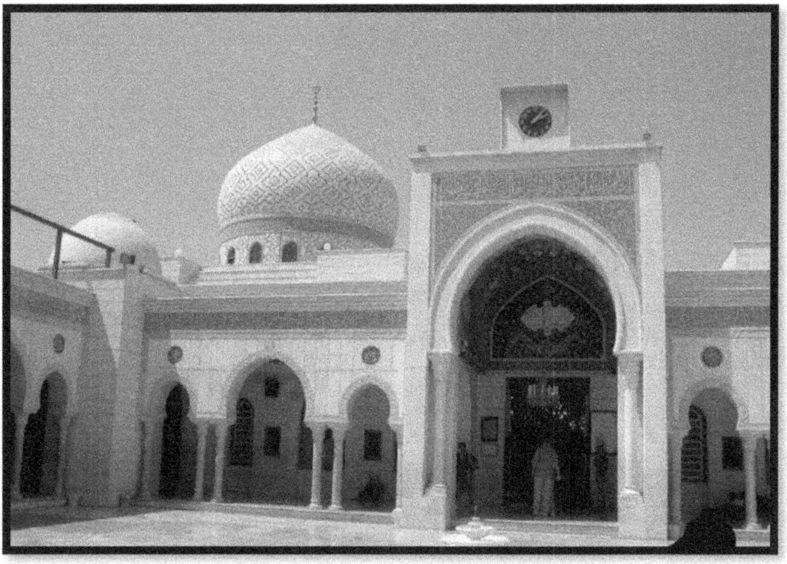

Lady Sakīna bint Ḥusayn ﷺ

Introduction to Lady Sakīna bint Ḥusayn ﷺ

Born to Imam Ḥusayn ﷺ and Lady Umm Rabāb ﷺ, Sakīna ﷺ - also known as Ruqayyah - was the youngest daughter of the 3rd Imam ﷺ and one of the youngest victims of the tragedy of Karbalā' and beyond.

As a child, she was vibrant, full of love and happiness, and even though she was very young when she left this world, Sakīna ﷺ was attached to the religion, loved to recite the Quran, and never missed her daily prayers.

There was a special bond between her and her uncle, Abūl Faḍl ʿAbbās ﷺ, and therefore, whenever she asked for anything, ʿAbbās ﷺ would ensure that he tried his best to fulfill her requests. In fact, on the way to Mecca from Madina, and then to Karbalā', ʿAbbās ﷺ accompanied the young Sakīna ﷺ in her caravan, and ensured that all her desires were attended to.

Seeing her father brutally killed on the Day of ʿĀshūrā', along with her family members and friends of the family further contributed to the grief and sorrow she felt on the painful journey to Kūfa, then Shām (Damascus).

In addition, the physical abuse and tortures she was subject to by the ruthless enemies of the Ahlul Bayt ﷺ led to her untimely death at the tender age of four or five in the dark, dreary prison in Damascus where she was laid to rest...

Ziyārah of Lady Sakīna bint Ḥusayn عليها السلام
Translated by Yasin T. Al-Jibouri

بِسْمِ اللّٰهِ الرَّحْمٰنِ الرَّحِيمِ

In the Name of Allah, the All-Compassionate, the All-Merciful

أَللّٰهُمَّ صَلِّ عَلٰى مُحَمَّدٍ وَّآلِ مُحَمَّدٍ وَعَجِّلْ فَرَجَهُمْ.

O Allah! Bless Muḥammad and the family of Muḥammad and hasten their relief.

أَلسَّلَامُ عَلَيْكِ يَا بِنْتَ النَّبِيِّ الْمُصْطَفٰى.

Peace be upon you, O daughter of the Chosen Prophet (al-Muṣṭafā).

أَلسَّلَامُ عَلَيْكِ يَا بِنْتَ الْوَلِيِّ الْمُرْتَضٰى.

Peace be upon you, O daughter of the Pleased Successor (al-Murtaḍā).

أَلسَّلَامُ عَلَيْكِ يَا بِنْتَ الْبَتُولِ الطَّاهِرَةِ فَاطِمَةَ الزَّهْرَآءِ.

Peace be upon you, O daughter of the Pure Maiden (al-Batūl), Fāṭima, the Radiant (al-Zahrā᾿).

أَلسَّلَامُ عَلَيْكِ يَا بِنْتَ خَدِيـجَةَ الْكُبْرَىٰ.

Peace be upon you, O daughter of Khadījah, the Grand-one
(al-Kubrā).

أَلسَّلَامُ عَلَيْكِ يَا بِنْتَ خَامِسِ أَصْحَابِ الْكِسَآءِ.

Peace be upon you, O daughter of the fifth of the *Aṣḥāb al-Kisā*. [30]

أَلسَّلَامُ عَلَيْكِ يَا فَلَذَةِ كَبْدٍ الْـمُرَمَّلِ بِالدِّمَآءِ.

Peace be upon you, O beloved soul who was totally covered
in blood.

أَلسَّلَامُ عَلَيْكِ يَا طِفْلَةَ الْمَقْتُولِ ظُلْمًا بِكَرْبَلَاءِ.

Peace be upon you, O child of the one who was unjustly
killed in Karbalā'.

أَلسَّلَامُ عَلَيْكِ يَا مُدَلَّلَةَ الْـحُسَيْنِ الشَّهِيدِ عَلَيْهِ السَّلَامُ.

Peace be upon you, O pampered one of Husayn, the martyr,
peace be upon him.

---

[30] *Aṣḥāb al-Kisā'* were the five people who had gathered under the blanket
or covering, and they were: the final Messenger of Allah, Prophet
Muḥammad ﷺ; his daughter, Fāṭima al-Zahrā ؑ; Commander of the
Faithful, Imam ʿAlī ؑ; and the Leaders of the Youth of Paradise - Imam
Ḥasan ؑ and Imam Ḥusayn ؑ.

وَرَحْـمَةُ اللهِ وَبَرَكَاتُهُ.

And may the mercy of Allah and His blessings (be upon you).

أَلسَّلَامُ عَلَيْكِ يَا رَبِيبَةَ بَيْتِ التُّقَى.

Peace be upon you, O one who was brought up in the house of piety.

أَلسَّلَامُ عَلَيْكِ يَا وَلِيدَةَ دَارِ الْإِبَاءِ.

Peace be upon you, O one who was born in the house of self-esteem.

أَلسَّلَامُ عَلَيْكِ يَا صَغِيرَةَ رُكْنِ الْهُدَى.

Peace be upon you, O small one of the pillars of guidance.

أَلسَّلَامُ عَلَيْكِ يَا شَهِيدَةَ الْـحُزْنِ وَالْبُكَاءِ.

Peace be upon you, O martyr of grieving and weeping.

أَلسَّلَامُ عَلَيْكِ يَا قَتِيلَةَ الصَّبْرِ عَلَى الْبَلَاءِ.

Peace be upon you, O one who was killed but still observed patience during the time of adversities.

أَلسَّلَامُ عَلَيْكِ يَا كَثِيرَةَ الشَّجَبِ وَالنِّدَآءِ.

Peace be upon you, O one who was much denounced and kept calling out.

وَرَحْمَةُ اللّٰهِ وَبَرَكَاتُهُ.

And may the mercy of Allah and His blessings (be upon you).

أَلسَّلَامُ عَلَى الْبَاكِيَةِ الشَّاكِيَةِ النَادِبَةِ.

Peace be upon the weeping, the complaining, the mourning one.

أَلسَّلَامُ عَلَى الْأَسِيرَةِ الْـمُنْتَحِبَةِ.

Peace be upon the wailing captive.

أَلسَّلَامُ عَلَى الْيَتِيمَةِ عِنْدَ الصِّبَا.

Peace be upon the one orphaned while still a child.

أَلسَّلَامُ عَلَى صَاحِبَةِ الْـحُزْنِ الْعَظِيمِ لِفَقْدِهَا مَنْ هُوَ بِهَا وَدُودٌ رَحِيمٌ.

Peace be upon the one who experienced great grief at the loss of the person who was affectionate and merciful towards her.

أَلسَّلَامُ عَلٰى ذَاتِ الْقَلْبِ الْكَظِيمِ.

Peace be upon the one with the grief-repressing heart.

أَلسَّلَامُ عَلٰى ذَاتِ الْعَيْنِ السَّكُوبِ.

Peace be upon the one with the over-flowing tearful eyes.

وَالْأَنَةُ الَّتِي تَقْطَعُ الْقُلُوبِ.

And the one who moaned such that tore the hearts apart.

بِـمَا تَضَافَرَتْ عَلَيْهَا النُّدُوبِ.

Due to the consecutive calamities which befell (upon her).

بِـمَا جَرَى فِي أَرْضِ الْكُرُوبِ.

Due to what happened (to her) in the land of afflictions.

وَرَحْمَةُ اللهِ وَبَرَكَاتُهُ.

And may the mercy of Allah and His blessings (be upon you).

أَلسَّلَامُ عَلٰى مَنْ بَالسِّيَاطِ لَوَّعُوهَا.

Peace be upon the one who was pained and whipped.

أَلسَّلَامُ عَلٰى الـمُنْحَنِيَةِ عَلٰى الْأَجْسَادِ الَّتِي صَرْعُوهَا.

Peace be upon the one who kept bending over bodies which they (the enemies) had killed.

أَلسَّلَامُ عَلٰى مَنْ عَنِ النِّيَاحَةِ مَنَعُوهَا.

Peace be upon the one whom they prevented from wailing and crying.

أَلسَّلَامُ عَلٰى الْأَسِيرَةِ الْمَقْطُوعَةِ.

Peace be upon the captive who was severed from [family] ties.

أَلسَّلَامُ عَلٰى الْـمَهْضُوْمَةِ الْـمَفْجُوعَةِ.

Peace be upon the wronged, the afflicted one.

أَلسَّلَامُ عَلٰى مَنْ حَالِهَا فِي شَجْبٍ وَعَوِيلٍ.

Peace be upon the one whose condition was [limited to] denouncing and wailing.

أَلسَّلَامُ عَلٰى مَنْ عُمْرِهَا بَعْدَ الْمُصَابِ قَلِيلٍ.

Peace be upon the one whose life after the calamity [in Karbalāʾ and beyond] was very short.

أَلسَّلَامُ عَلٰى مَنْ غَابَ عَنْهَا الْـحَامِي وَالْكَفِيلِ.

Peace be upon the one from whom the protector and guardian was absent.

وَرَحْمَةُ اللّٰهِ وَبَرَكَـاتُهُ.

And may the mercy of Allah and His blessings (be upon you).

سَلَامِي لِمَنْ شَهَادَتُهَا بِالنَّازِلَةِ الْكُبْرٰى.

My salutation goes to the one who was martyred in the supreme catastrophe.

وَحُزْنِي لِمَنْ مُصِيبَتُهَا فَجِيعَةٌ عُظْمٰى،

I grieve for the one whose tribulation was a great calamity,

حَيْثُ جَنَّ عَلَيْهَا الظَّلَامِ،

When the darkness overwhelmed her,

وَقَدْ أَدْخَلَتْ خَرَابَةِ الشَّامِ،

And when she was lodged in the house of ruin in Shām (Damascus),

مَعَ عَمَّتِهَا الَّتِي جُـمِعَتْ وَلِّهَا الْأَيْتَامِ،

Who along with her aunt, gathered the orphans around her,

وَحَيْثُ سُكِنَتْ مِنَ النَّوَاحِ،

And when the wailers [amongst them] were forced to remain silent,

وَهَدَأَتْ أَنْفَاسَ الْـحُزْنِ وَالصِّيَاحِ،

And when the breaths of grief and wailing calmed down,

وَبَاتُوا مُلْتَمِسِينَ الصَّبَاحِ،

And when they spent the night seeking the dawn,

فَفَزَعْتِي يَا رُقَيَّةَ مِنَ الْمَنَامِ،

So you, O Ruqayyah, were frightened in your sleep,

وَبَدَا مِنْكِ النَّوْحِ وَالْإِهْتِضَامِ،

And you took to wailing and oppression,

وَنَدَبْتِ أَبَاكِ بِأَشْجىٰ الْكَلَامِ.

And mourning your father with the most sombre of words.

فَلَمَّا وَصَلَ الصَّوْتُ إِلىٰ يَزِيدِ (لَعَنَهُ اللّٰهُ)،

When the sound [the voice of Sakīna] reached Yazīd (may the curse of Allah be upon him),

أُمِرَ بِالطَّشْتِ وَفِيهِ رَأْسِ الشَّهِيدِ.

He ordered that a washbowl be brought in which contained the head of the martyr [Imam Ḥusayn ﷺ].

وَبَيْتُ مَا كَانَ يَرْمِيَ وَيُرِيدُ،

And he [Yazīd] hid his thoughts and what he wanted to do,

وَبَدَأَ بِالشَّمَاتَةِ وَالظُّلْمِ الشَّدِيدِ،

And he started expressing elation at the calamity, showing such a great injustice,

نَاوِيًا تَقْطِيعُ قَلْبِكِ بِـمَا يَفُتُّ الصَّخْرِ وَالْـحَدِيدَ،

With the intention of cutting your heart into pieces by doing something through which even stone and iron would crumble,

فَخِيَمِ الْـحُزْنُ عَلَى النِّسْوَةِ الْهَاشِمِيَّةِ،

Grief cast its shadow upon the ladies of the Hashemites,

حِينَمَا رَأَيْنَ رَأْسُ صَاحِبِ الْغَيْرَةِ وَالْـحَمِيَّةِ،

On seeing the head of the man of fervour and manliness [Imam Ḥusayn ﷺ],

وَصِرْتِ أَنْتِ تَنْظُرِينَ إِلَىٰ تَاجِ الْعِتْرَةِ الْأَبِيَّةِ،

And you kept looking at the crown of the dignified family [of Prophet Muḥammad ﷺ],

وَقَدْ دَهَاكِ الْمَنْظَرِ يَا رُقَيَّةَ،

And certainly, the sight shook you, O Ruqayyah,

وَقَدْ تَسَرْبَلَتْ بِالدِّمَآءِ شَيْبَتَهُ،

And certainly, as the blood drenched his beard,

وَتَنَكَّثَتْ بِالْقَضِيبِ شَفَتُهُ،

And his lip was hard pressed with the iron rod,

وَشَحْبَةٌ مِنَ الْعَطَشِ وَجْنَتُهُ،

And his cheeks had turned pale due to the thirst,

وَقَدْ شَخَصَتْ عَيْنَاهُ إِلىٰ السَّمَآءِ،

And his eyes were fixed on the heavens,

حِينَمَا وَجَّهَ ذَاكَ النِّدَآءِ:

And he directed this address:

إِلٰهِي تَرَكْتُ الْـخَلْقَ طُرًّا فِي هَوَاكَ،

"O Lord! I have abandoned all of creation while in Your love,

وَأَيْتَمْتُ الْعِيَالِ لِكَـيْ أَرَاكَ،

And I have orphaned my children so that I may see You,

فَلَوْ قَطَعْتَنِي فِي الْـحُبِّ إِرْبًا،

Therefore, if You cut me into pieces while in (Your) love,

لَمَا مَالِ الْفُؤَادِ إِلىٰ سِوَاكَ.

My heart will never prefer anyone over You."

أَلسَّلَامُ عَلٰى مَنْ لِسَانِ حَالِهَا يَقْطَعُ الْقُلُوبِ.

Peace be upon the one whose condition [when one hears it] cuts the hearts into pieces.

أَلسَّلَامُ عَلٰى صَاحِبَةِ الْـخِطَابِ الْعَجِيبِ،

Peace be upon the one who delivered an amazing speech,

لِصَاحِبِ الْـخَدِّ التَّرِيبِ،

In defence of the one whose cheeks were ruffled with the dust,

أَبِيكِ أَبَا عَبْدِ اللهِ الْـحُسَيْنِ عَلَيْهِ السَّلَامُ.

Your father, Abā ʿAbdillāh, al-Ḥusayn, peace be upon him.

حِينَ نَادَيْتِ: يَا أَبَتَاهْ! مَنْ خَضَبَ الشَّيْبِ الْعَفِيفِ؟

It was then that you called out: "O father! Who drenched the virtuous beard with blood?

مَنْ قَطَعَ النَّحْرِ الشَّرِيفِ؟

Who severed the holy neck?

مَنْ أَيْتَمَنِي عَلَى صِغَرِ سِنِّي؟

Who made me an orphan while I am still a child?"

إِلَيْكِ يَا رُقَيَّةَ إِنِّي:

To you, O Ruqayyah, I express my puzzlement:

أَحَارُ فِيمَا تُبْدِينَهُ مِنَ النَّشِيجِ؟

How can I describe your sobbing?

أَلسَّلَامُ عَلَى مَنِ انْكَبَّتْ عَلَى رَأْسِ أَبِيهَا شَائِقَةً.

Peace be upon the one who fell on the head of her father anxiously.

أَلسَّلَامُ عَلٰى مَنْ حُضِنَتْ رَأْسِ حُمَّاهَا ضَآئِقَةً.

Peace be upon the one whose feverish head was hugged.

أَلسَّلَامُ عَلٰى مَنْ أَحْوَالِـهَا عَنْهَا نَاطِقَةً.

Peace be upon the one whose condition spoke for her.

أَلسَّلَامُ عَلٰى رُوحِكِ الصَّاعِدَةِ بَعْدَ وُقُوعِكِ عَلٰى الرَّأْسِ الشَّرِيفِ.

Peace be upon your ascending soul after you fell on the noble head [of your father, Imam Ḥusayn ﷺ].

أَلسَّلَامُ عَلٰى جَوَارِحِكِ الذَّابِلَةِ مِنَ السِّيَرِ الْـحَثِيثِ.

Peace be upon your withering limbs due to incessant walking.

أَلسَّلَامُ عَلٰى الرُّوحِ الْمُوَدَّعَةِ لِلجَّوَارِحِ الْـمُتَحَسِّرَةِ.

Peace be upon the soul that bade farewell to the sighing senses.

أَلسَّلَامُ عَلٰى الْـجَسَدِ الْمُفَارِقِ لِلرُّوحِ الْـمُتَفَطِّرَةِ.

Peace be upon the body - the fractured soul of which departed [from it].

أَلسَّلَامُ عَلَى مَنْ أَبْكَتِ النِّسَآءِ مُصِيبَتَهَا،

Peace be upon the one who caused the women [of the caravan] to weep,

لِهَوْلِ مَا رَأَوْهُ مِنْهَا وَلِعِظَمِ مَا جَرَى عَلَيْهَا،

Due to the horrific site of what they saw, and because of the gravity of what transpired,

حِينَمَا جِيءَ بِرَأْسِ أَبِيهَا إِلَيْهَا.

On account of what happened to her when her father's head was brought to her.

فَقَالَ الْإِمَامُ زَيْنُ الْعَابِدِينَ عَلَيْهِ السَّلَامُ: إِرْفَعُوهَا فَلَقَدْ فَارَقَتْ رُوْحُهَا الدُّنْيَا...

Imam Zaynul ʿĀbidīn, peace be upon him, said: "Lift her, for her soul has departed from this world..."

فَرَفَعُوكِ، وَإِذَا أَنْتِ مَيْتَةٌ.

So, they lifted you, and you had passed away.

أَلسَّلَامُ عَلَى مَنْ زَادَتْ مُصَابَ آلِ الْبَيْتِ.

Peace be upon the one who intensified the calamity of the People of the Household [Ahlul Bayt ﷺ].

أَلسَّلَامُ عَلَيْكِ يَا صَاحِبَةَ النَّفْسِ الْأَبِيَّةِ.

Peace be upon you, O the one with the self-esteemed soul.

أَلسَّلَامُ عَلَيْكِ يَا سَلِيلَةَ الْحُسَيْنِ الْمَسْبِيَّةِ.

Peace be upon you, O the captive descendant of Ḥusayn.

أَلسَّلَامُ عَلَى ابْنَةِ الْأَنْوَارِ الْمُحَمَّدِيَّةُ.

Peace be upon you, O daughter of the Muḥammadī celestial lights.

أَلسَّلَامُ عَلَيْكِ يَا غُصْنَ الشَّجَرَةِ الْعَلَوِيَّةِ الْفَاطِمِيَّةِ.

Peace be upon you, O branch of the ʿAlawīyyah and Fāṭimīyyah Tree.

يَا صَغِيرَةَ الْحُسَيْنِ ... يَا رُقَيَّةَ،

O little one of Ḥusayn ... O Ruqayyah,

وَرَحْمَةُ اللّٰهِ وَبَرَكَاتُهُ.

May the mercy of Allah and His blessings (be upon you).

لَقَدْ عَظُمَتْ مُصَآبِنَا بِكِ يَا ابْنَةَ الْحُسَيْنِ،

Certainly, our calamities have been aggravated because of you, O daughter of Ḥusayn,

وَشَخَصَتْ أَعْيُنُنَا إِلَيكِ بِالدَّمَعِ السَّخِينِ،

And our eyes are fixed upon you with warm tears,

وَشَحَبَتْ أَلْوَانُنَا بِنَشِيجِ الْوَالِهِ الْـحَزِينِ،

And the colours of our faces have been robbed by wailing (our faces have become pale),

وَتَكَبَّدَتْ قُلُوبَنَا مِنْ أَسْهُمِ الْـحِقْدُ الدَّفِينِ،

And our hearts have suffered due to the [proverbial] darts [which have struck them due to the numerous tribulations which you endured],

لآلِ أُمَيَّةَ الظَّالِمِين.

[Of the hidden animosity] from the oppressive ones of the Umayyad Dynasty.

وَتَـجَمَّعَتْ أَرْوَاحُنَا هُنَا بِـحَضْرَتِكِ بِالشَّوْقِ وَالْـحَنِينِ
وَبِالْزَفْرَةِ وَالْأَنِينِ.

Our souls have gathered here in your presence with anxiety, affection, sighs, and moaning.

تَنْدُبُ الْآلِ الطَّاهِرِين،

The purified [Ahlul Bayt ﷺ] are mourning,

وَتَشْكُو لَوْعَةَ الْمُصَابِ،

And are complaining about the anguish,

وَشِدَّةَ الْأَكْتِئَابِ،

And severity of the grief,

وَعُسْرَةَ الْعَذَابِ،

And hardship of the pain,

وَغُصَّةَ الْفِرَاقِ،

And sorrow of the separation,

وَحَرَارَةَ الْإِشْتِيَاقِ.

And warmth of the affection.

وَنَرْجُوا مِنَ اللّٰهُ بِكُمْ لَنَا عِوَضًا،

And we plead to Allah to compensate us for having lost you,

بِكَثْرَةِ الثَّوَابِ،

With the abundance of rewards,

وَحُسْنِ الْمَآبِ.

And a goodly return to Him.

نَسْأَلُ اللهَ بِالشَّأْنِ الَّذِي لَدَيْكِ،

We plead to Allah through the status which you enjoy with Him,

وَبِالشَّرَفِ الَّذِي بَيْنَ يَدَيْكِ،

And through the honour which is before you,

وَبِالْمَقَامِ الَّذِي تُشْرِقُ مِنْهُ أَنْوَارُكِ،

And through the place from which your lights shine,

أَنْ تَكُونِي شَفِيعَةً لِلْمُذْنِبِ الْحَقِيرِ،

That you will intercede on behalf of this lowly sinner,

وَاللَّآئِذِ الْمُسْتَجِيرِ،

And the fugitive seeker of a safe haven,

وَالْمُضْطَرِّ الْكَسِيرِ،

And the heart-broken, helpless supporter (of you all),

مِنْ شِيعَتِكُمْ وَمُحِبِّيكُمْ،

From among your followers and your lovers,

أَلتَّائِبِينَ إِلَىٰ الْعَلِيمِ الْبَصِيرِ،

Who repent to the All-Knowing, the All-Seeing,

بِأَنْ يَنَالُ بِكُمْ تَـمَامَ ثَوَابِ الزِّيَارَاتِ،

So, they may attain, through you [the Ahlul Bayt ﷺ], the perfect rewards of the visitation *(ziyārah)*,

وَيُفْلِحُ بِآخِرَتِهِ بِـمُضَاعَفَةِ الْمَثُوبَاتِ،

And so they may achieve success in the Hereafter when their rewards are doubled,

وَغُفْرَانِ الْـخَطِيئَاتِ،

And have the sins forgiven,

إِنَّ رَبِّي بِـمَا يَشَآءُ لَطِيفٌ.

Surely, my Lord is All-Gracious in things.

وَهُوَبِكُمْ مُـجِيبٌ عُطُوفٌ،

And He is with you [O Ahlul Bayt ﷺ] - the One who compassionately answers the prayers,

وَهُوَلَكُمْ رَحِيمٌ رَؤُوفٌ.

And He is, to you [Ahlul Bayt ﷺ], All-Merciful, All-Compassionate.

وَالسَّلَامُ عَلَيْكُمْ سَادَتِي،

And peace be upon you, my masters,

وَرَحْمَةُ اللّٰهِ وَبَرَكَاتُهُ.

and may the mercy of Allah and His blessings (be upon you).

أَشْهَدُ أَنَّكُمْ تَحَمَّلْتُمُ الْمُصَابِ،

I testify that you tolerated whatever afflictions came upon you,

وَأَنَّكُمْ أَحْيَاءٌ بِنَصِّ الْكِتَابِ،

And that you are [currently] alive according to the text of the Book (the Noble Quran),

حَيْثُ قَالَ سَرِيعُ الْحِسَابِ:

Where the One Who is Swift in Reckoning says:

﴿وَلَا تَحْسَبَنَّ الَّذِينَ قُتِلُوا فِي سَبِيلِ اللّٰهِ أَمْوَاتًا بَلْ أَحْيَاءٌ عِنْدَ رَبِّهِمْ يُرْزَقُونَ.﴾

"And do not reckon those who are killed in the way of Allah as dead. Nay! They are living with their Lord, receiving sustenance."[31]

أَللّٰهُمَّ صَلِّ عَلَى مُحَمَّدٍ وَآلِ مُحَمَّدٍ.

O Allah! Bless Muḥammad and the Progeny of Muḥammad.

---

[31] Quran, Sūrah Āle 'Imrān (3), Verse 69.

أَللّٰهُمَّ إِنِّي أَسْأَلُكِ بِالْمُصِيبَةِ الْعُظْمَى وَبِالنَّازِلَةِ الْكُبْرَى،

O Allah! I plead to You through the medium of the great calamity and the grand affliction,

وَبِـمَا جَرَى فِي كَرْبَلَآءَ،

And what transpired in Karbalāʾ,

أَنْ تُصَلِّيَ عَلٰى مُـحَمَّدٍ وَّآلِ مُـحَمَّدٍ،

That You bless Muḥammad and the Progeny of Muḥammad,

وَأَنْ تَقِيَنَا شَرِّ الْأَسْوَآءِ،

And that You spare us the ills of everything that is evil,

وَتَهُبُّ لَنَا الظُّلَامَاتِ،

And to overlook for us our injustices,

وَتُقَوِّيَنَا عَلٰى مُجَاهَدَةِ الْمُنْكِرَاتِ.

And to strengthen us so that we may resist the committing of what You abhor.

أَللّٰهُمَّ إِنَا نَتَوَجَّهُ إِلَيْكَ بِصُرْعَةِ رُقَيَّةَ الْيَتِيمَةُ،

O Allah! We direct ourselves to You through the medium of the devastation that killed Ruqayyah, the orphan,

وَبَهَاتِيكَ الْفَاجِعَةِ الْعَظِيمَةِ،

And through the medium of the momentous calamity,

وَبِتِلْكَ الْمُصِيبَةِ الشَّدِيدَةِ،

And through the medium of the severe affliction,

وَمَا نَزَلَ بِالْعِتْرَةِ الـمَجِيدَةِ،

And through the suffering of the glorified family [of Prophet Muḥammad ﷺ],

وَبِـجَاهِ رُوْحَهَا الطَّاهِرَةِ،

And through the medium of her [Sakīna's] pure soul,

وَجَوَارِحِهَا الصَّابِرَةِ،

And her patient limbs,

وَأَدْمُعِهَا السَخِيَّةِ،

And her generous tears,

وَبِـمَا هِيَ عِنْدَكِ مَرْضِيَّةً.

And through her (status) which is pleasing to You.

أَنْ تَقْضِيَ حَاجَاتِنَا وَحَاجَاتِ الْمُؤْمِنِينَ وَالْمُؤْمِنَاتِ

That you fulfill our needs, and the needs of the believing men and the believing women.

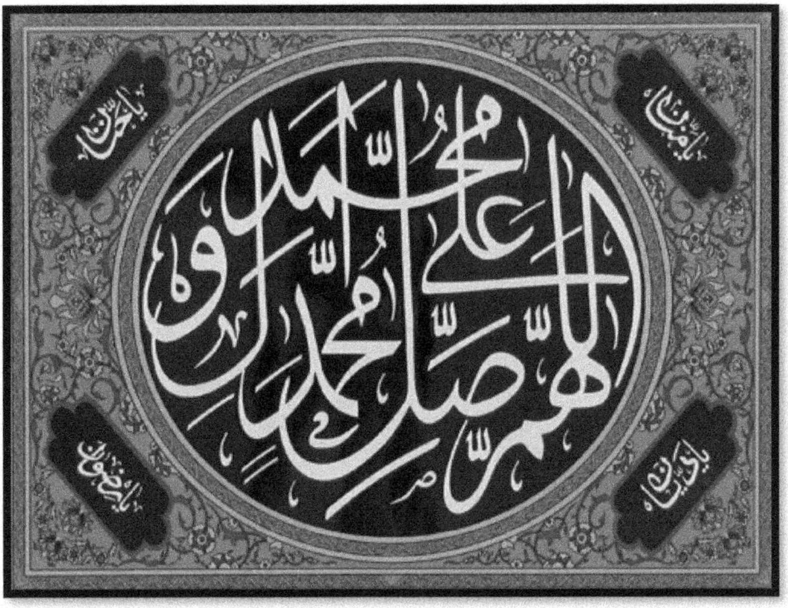
اللهم صل على محمد وآل محمد

Ziyārat Āle Yāsīn

Introduction to Ziyārat Āle Yāsīn

With the 12th Imam in *ghaybah* (occultation) - we are not able to be in direct contact with him on our conditions - however, he is free to be in contact with those whom he wishes. Therefore, one of the ways we can keep in daily contact with Imam al-Mahdi عجل الله تعالى فرجه الشريف is through the various supplications and *ziyārāt* which the immaculate ones عليهم السلام - especially the 12th Imam عجل الله تعالى فرجه الشريف - have taught to us.

Imam al-Mahdi عجل الله تعالى فرجه الشريف does not have a fixed location where he is during the period of occultation and there is no specific *masjid* or location that we can turn our attention towards. However according to the narrations, we have been told that he performs *Ḥajj* every year, and that he frequents *Masjid al-Sahlah* in the city of Kūfa in Iraq as well as *Masjid Jamkarān* in Qum in Iran. However other than these few locations which we see noted about him and his activities, there are no other indicators in regard to his specific daily whereabouts.

During these troubling days and nights when our Imam is "away" from us, or as some scholars have mentioned - us being distanced from him - one of the most beautiful ways to speak with him is through *Ziyārat Āle Yāsīn.*

This *Ziyārat* consists of two parts: the main text of the *Ziyārat*, followed by a *Duʿāʾ* - both of which have been taught to us by the 12th Imam عجل الله تعالى فرجه الشريف himself.

One of the most praiseworthy things which we can do during the era of occultation is to verbally proclaim our religious beliefs so that we can remain free from the whisperings of Shayṭān. One of the ways to do this is to regularly recite this *Ziyārat* in which we make the 12th Imam ﷺ a witness to our beliefs.

The introductory portion of this *Ziyārat* begins by greeting the Imam ﷺ with many of his titles, followed by a proclamation of the belief in One God - Allah ﷻ, Prophet Muḥammad ﷺ, and the 12 Imams ﷺ - in which we mention each one of them by name, and how they are Proofs of Allah ﷻ on the Earth. Thereafter, we testify to the reality and belief of our creed in Paradise, Hell, and all other truths of the Hereafter.

A constant recitation of this *Ziyārat* with understanding and acceptance of its contents can help a believer attain deep cognizance *(maʿrifah)*, servitude *(ʿubudiyyah)*, and love *(maḥabbah)* of Allah ﷻ. It can be recited on any day, at any time.

May the 12th Imam ﷺ hear our humble pleas, through the permission of Allah ﷻ, and be there to help us when we turn to him in our difficult moments. May we have the honour of meeting our living Imam ﷺ through reciting this *Ziyārat* with complete focus, contemplation, and understanding.

Ziyārat Āle Yāsīn

Translated by Saleem Bhimji

بِسْمِ اللّٰهِ الرَّحْمٰنِ الرَّحِيمِ

In the Name of Allah, the All-Compassionate, the All-Merciful

سَلَامٌ عَلٰى آلِ يٰسٓ.

Peace be upon the progeny of Yāsīn (family of Prophet Muḥammad ﷺ - the Ahlul Bayt ﷺ).

أَلسَّلَامُ عَلَيْكَ يَا دَاعِيَ اللّٰهِ وَرَبَّانِيَّ آيَاتِهِ.

Peace be upon you, O the Caller of Allah, and Place of Manifestation of His Signs.

أَلسَّلَامُ عَلَيْكَ يَا بَابَ اللّٰهِ وَدَيَّانَ دِينِهِ.

Peace be upon you, O the Door of Allah, and the Devout One of His Religion.

أَلسَّلَامُ عَلَيْكَ يَا خَلِيفَةَ اللّٰهِ وَنَاصِرَ حَقِّهِ.

Peace be upon you, O the Vicegerent of Allah and the Helper of His Truth.

أَلسَّلَامُ عَلَيْكَ يَا حُجَّةَ اللّٰهِ وَدَلِيلَ إِرَادَتِهِ.

Peace be upon you, O the Proof of Allah and the Symbol of His Ordinance.

أَلسَّلَامُ عَلَيْكَ يَا تَالِيَ كِتَابِ اللّٰهِ وَتَرْجُمَانَهُ.

Peace be upon you, O the Reciter of Allah's Book and its Interpreter.

أَلسَّلَامُ عَلَيْكَ فِي آنَاءِ لَيْلِكَ وَأَطْرَافِ نَهَارِكَ.

Peace be upon you in your night and your day.

أَلسَّلَامُ عَلَيْكَ يَا بَقِيَّةَ اللّٰهِ فِي أَرْضِهِ.

Peace be upon you, O the Remnant of Allah (the One who is remaining) on His Earth.

أَلسَّلَامُ عَلَيْكَ يَا مِيثَاقَ اللّٰهِ الَّذِي أَخَذَهُ وَوَكَّدَهُ.

Peace be upon you, O the Covenant of Allah, which He took, and He affirmed.

أَلسَّلَامُ عَلَيْكَ يَا وَعْدَ اللّٰهِ الَّذِي ضَمِنَهُ.

Peace be upon you, O the Promise of Allah which He guaranteed.

أَلسَّلَامُ عَلَيْكَ أَيُّهَا الْعَلَمُ الْـمَنْصُوبُ،

Peace by upon you, O the Raised Flag,

وَالْعِلْمُ الْـمَصْـبُوبُ،

And the One who is Moulded with Knowledge,

وَالْغَوْثُ وَالرَّحْمَةُ الْوَاسِعَةُ،

And the Help, and the Far-Reaching Mercy,

وَعْدًا غَيْرَ مَكْذُوبٍ.

And the promise which is not a lie.

أَلسَّلَامُ عَلَيْكَ حِينَ تَقُومُ.

Peace be upon you while you are standing.

أَلسَّلَامُ عَلَيْكَ حِينَ تَقْعُدُ.

Peace be upon you while you are sitting.

أَلسَّلَامُ عَلَيْكَ حِينَ تَقْرَأُ وَتُـبَيِّنُ.

Peace be upon you when you are reading and explaining (the Quran).

أَلسَّلَامُ عَلَيْكَ حِينَ تُصَلِّي وَتَـقْنُتُ.

Peace be upon you when you are praying and supplicating.

أَلسَّلَامُ عَلَيْكَ حِينَ تَرْكَعُ وَتَسْجُدُ.

Peace be upon you when you are bowing (in *rukūʿ*) and prostrating (in *sajdah*).

أَلسَّلَامُ عَلَيْكَ حِينَ تُـهَلِّلُ وَتُكَبِّرُ.

Peace be upon you when you are announcing the *Tahlīl* (saying: There is no god but Allah); and the *Takbīr* (saying: Allah is Greater [than can be described]).

أَلسَّلَامُ عَلَيْكَ حِينَ تَحْمَدُ وَتَسْتَغْفِرُ.

Peace be upon you when you are praising (Allah) and seeking forgiveness.

أَلسَّلَامُ عَلَيْكَ حِينَ تُصْبِحُ وَتُـمْسِي.

Peace be upon you when you enter the morning and the evening.

أَلسَّلَامُ عَلَيْكَ فِي اللَّيْلِ إِذَا يَغْشىٰ وَالنَّهَارِ إِذَا تَجَلَّى.

Peace be upon you in the night when it envelops, and the day when it becomes manifest.

أَلسَّلَامُ عَلَيْكَ أَيُّهَا الْإِمَامُ الْـمَأْمُونُ.

Peace be upon you, O the Protected Leader.

أَلسَّلَامُ عَلَيْكَ أَيُّهَا الْـمُقَدَّمُ الْـمَأْمُولُ.

Peace be upon you, O the One whose coming is hoped for.

أَلسَّلَامُ عَلَيْكَ بِجَوَامِعِ السَّلَامِ.

Peace be upon you with the collection of all the salutations.

أُشْهِدُكَ يَا مَوْلَايَ أَنِّـي أَشْهَدُ أَنْ لَا إِلٰهَ إِلَّا اللّٰهُ وَحْدَهُ لَا شَرِيكَ لَـهُ.

I call you as a witness, O my Master, that certainly I testify that there is no god except Allah, He is alone, there is no partner with Him.

وَأَنَّ مُحَمَّدًا عَبْدُهُ وَرَسُوْلُهُ لَا حَبِيبَ إِلَّا هُوَ وَأَهْلُهُ.

And (I testify) that indeed Muḥammad is His servant and His Messenger; there is no beloved except him and his progeny.

وَأُشْهِدُكَ يَا مَوْلَايَ أَنَّ عَلِيًّا أَمِيرَ الْـمُؤْمِنِينَ حُجَّتُهُ،

And I call you as a witness, O my Master, that certainly ʿAlī, the Commander of the Faithful, is His Proof,

وَالْـحَسَنَ حُجَّتُهُ، وَالْـحُسَيْنَ حُجَّتُهُ،

And Ḥasan is His Proof, and Ḥusayn is His Proof,

وَعَلِيَّ بْنَ الْـحُسَيْنِ حُجَّتُهُ،

And ʿAlī, son of Ḥusayn, is His Proof,

وَمُحَمَّدَ بْنَ عَلِيٍّ حُجَّتُهُ،

And Muḥammad, son of ʿAlī, is His Proof,

وَجَعْفَرَ بْنَ مُحَمَّدٍ حُجَّتُهُ،

And Jaʿfar, son of Muḥammad, is His Proof,

وَمُوسَىٰ بْنَ جَعْفَرٍ حُجَّتُهُ،

And Mūsā, son of Jaʿfar, is His Proof,

وَعَلِيَّ بْنَ مُوسَىٰ حُجَّتُهُ،

And ʿAlī, son of Mūsā, is His Proof,

وَمُحَمَّدَ بْنَ عَلِيٍّ حُجَّتُهُ،

And Muḥammad, son of ʿAlī, is His Proof,

وَعَلِيَّ بْنَ مُحَمَّدٍ حُجَّتُهُ،

And ʿAlī, son of Muḥammad, is His Proof,

وَالْـحَسَنَ بْنَ عَلِيٍّ حُجَّتُهُ،

And Ḥasan, son of ʿAlī, is His Proof,

وَأَشْهَدُ أَنَّكَ حُجَّةُ اللّٰهِ.

And I testify that indeed you are the Proof of Allah.

أَنْتُمُ الْأَوَّلُ وَالْآخِرُ.

You (all) are the first and the last.

وَأَنَّ رَجْعَتَكُمْ حَقٌّ لَا رَيْبَ فِيهَا، يَوْمَ لَا يَنْفَعُ نَفْسًا إِيمَانُهَا لَمْ تَكُنْ آمَنَتْ مِنْ قَبْلُ أَوْ كَسَبَتْ فِي إِيمَانِهَا خَيْرًا.

And surely your return is a truth, there is no doubt in it, (on) the Day when (the) belief of no one will benefit them who did not previously believe, and (did not) acquire goodness through their belief.

وَأَنَّ الْمَوْتَ حَقٌّ،

And indeed, death is (an inescapable) reality (the truth),

وَأَنَّ نَاكِرًا وَنَكِيرًا حَقٌّ،

And indeed (the questioning of) *Nākir* and *Nakīr* is a reality,

وَأَشْهَدُ أَنَّ النَّشْرَ حَقٌّ،

And I testify that indeed the dispersion (on the Day of Judgement) is a reality,

وَالْبَعْثَ حَقٌّ،

And the resurrection is a reality,

وَأَنَّ الصِّرَاطَ حَقٌّ،

And indeed the (narrow) path (over Hell) is a reality,

وَالْـمِرْصَادَ حَقٌّ،

And the place of observation is a reality,

وَالْـمِيزَانَ حَقٌّ،

And the (measuring of the) scales is a reality,

وَالْـحَشْرَ حَقٌّ،

And the gathering (of all human beings) is a reality,

وَالْـحِسَابَ حَقٌّ،

And the accounting (of deeds) is a reality,

وَالْـجَـنَّةَ وَالنَّارَ حَقٌّ،

And Paradise and Hell are a reality,

وَالْوَعْدَ وَالْوَعِيدَ بِهِمَا حَقٌّ.

And the promise and threat of them both is a reality.

يَا مَوْلَايَ شَقِيَ مَنْ خَالَـفَكُمْ،

O my Master, one who opposes you all is wretched,

وَسَعِدَ مَنْ أَطَاعَكُمْ.

And the one who obeys you all is successful.

فَاشْهَدْ عَلٰى مَا أَشْهَدْتُكَ عَلَيْهِ.

Then testify whatever I made you a witness upon.

وَأَنَا وَلِيٌّ لَكَ بَرِيـءٌ مِنْ عَدُوِّكَ.

And I am a friend of yours, distanced from your enemy.

فَالْـحَقُّ مَا رَضِـيتُمُوهُ،

So, the truth is whatever you are pleased with,

وَالْبَاطِلُ مَا أَسْخَطْـتُمُوهُ،

And the falsehood is whatever you are angry with,

وَالْـمَعْرُوفُ مَا أَمَرْتُمْ بِهِ،

And the goodness is whatever you all have ordered,

وَالْـمُنْكَرُ مَا نَـهَـيْتُمْ عَنْهُ.

And the evil is whatever you all have prohibited.

فَنَفْسِي مُؤْمِنَةٌ بِاللهِ وَحْدَهُ لَا شَرِيكَ لَهُ،

So, I am a believer in Allah, the One, He has no partner,

وَبِرَسُولِهِ وَبِأَمِيرِ الْمُؤْمِنِينَ وَبِكُمْ يَا مَوْلَايَ،

And (I am a believer) in His Messenger, and in the Commander of the Faithful, and in all of you, O my Master,

أَوَّلِكُمْ وَآخِرِكُمْ.

The first among you and the last among you.

وَنُصْرَتِي مُعَدَّةٌ لَكُمْ،

And my help is ready for you all,

وَمَوَدَّتِي خَالِصَةٌ لَكُمْ.

And my love is purely for you all.

آمِينَ آمِينَ.

Amīn! Amīn! (Accept! Accept! [whatever I have asked for]).

The following supplication (Du'ā') should then be recited to complete this Ziyārat:

أَللّٰهُمَّ إِنِّي أَسْأَلُكَ أَنْ تُصَلِّيَ عَلى مُحَمَّدٍ نَبِيِّ رَحْمَتِكَ،

O Allah, surely, I ask You to send blessings upon Muḥammad - the Prophet of Your Mercy,

وَكَلِمَةِ نُورِكَ.

And the Word of Your Light.

وَأَنْ تَـمْلَأَ قَلْـبِي نُورَ الْيَقِينِ،

And (I ask You to) fill my heart with the light of certainty,

وَصَدْرِي نُورَ الْإِيـمَانِ،

And my chest with the light of faith,

وَفِكْرِي نُورَ النِّيَّاتِ،

And my thinking with the light of (good) intentions,

وَعَزْمِي نُورَ الْعِلْمِ،

And my determination with the light of knowledge,

وَقُوَّتِي نُورَ الْعَمَلِ،

And my strength with the light of action,

وَلِسَانِي نُورَ الصِّدْقِ،

And my tongue with the light of truthfulness,

وَدِيـنِي نُورَ الْبَصَآئِرِ مِنْ عِنْدِكَ،

And my religion with the light of understanding from You,

وَبَصَرِي نُورَ الضِّـيَآءِ،

And my vision with the light of illumination,

وَسَمْعِي نُورَ الْـحِكْمَةِ،

And my hearing with the light of wisdom,

وَمَوَدَّتِي نُورَ الْـمُوَالاَةِ لِـمُحَمَّدٍ وَآلِهِ عَلَيْهِمُ السَّلَامُ،

And my love with the light of sincere loyalty to Muḥammad and his progeny, peace be upon all of them,

حَتّٰى أَلْقَاكَ وَقَدْ وَفَيْتُ بِعَهْدِكَ وَمِيثَاقِكَ.

Until I meet You having certainly fulfilled (my duty to) Your promise and Your covenant.

فَتُغَشِّيَنِي رَحْمَتَكَ، يَا وَلِيُّ يَا حَمِيدُ.

So, cover me with Your Mercy, O Master! O Praiseworthy!

أَللّٰـهُمَّ صَلِّ عَلَىٰ مُحَمَّدٍ حُجَّتِكَ فِي أَرْضِكَ،

O Allah, send Your blessings upon Muḥammad, Your Proof (the 12th Imam عجل الله تعالى فرجه الشريف) on Your Earth,

وَخَلِيفَتِكَ فِي بِلَادِكَ،

And Your Vicegerent over Your Lands,

وَالدَّاعِي إِلَىٰ سَبِيلِكَ،

And the Caller towards Your Way,

وَالْقَآئِمِ بِقِسْطِكَ،

And the Establisher of Your Justice,

وَالسَّآئِرِ بِأَمْرِكَ،

And the One who follows Your Command,

وَلِيِّ الْمُؤْمِنِينَ وَبَوَارِ الْكَافِرِينَ،

And the Master of the Believers, and the (cause of) Ruin of the Disbelievers,

وَمُجَلِّي الظُّلْمَةِ وَمُنِيرِ الْحَقِّ،

And the Enlightener of the Darkness, and the Illuminator of the Truth,

وَالنَّاطِقِ بِالْحِكْمَةِ وَالصِّدْقِ،

And the Speaker with Wisdom and Truthfulness,

وَكَلِمَتِكَ التَّآمَّةِ فِي أَرْضِكَ،

And Your Complete Word on Your Earth,

أَلْمُرْتَقِبِ الْخَآئِفِ،

The Anxious Anticipator,

وَالْوَلِيِّ النَّاصِحِ،

And the Counselling Master,

سَفِينَةِ النَّجَاةِ،

The Ship of Salvation,

وَعَلَمِ الْهُدىٰ،

And the Flag of Guidance,

وَنُورِ أَبْصَارِ الْوَرىٰ،

And the Light of the Peoples' Sight,

وَخَيْرِ مَنْ تَقَمَّصَ وَارْتَدىٰ،

And the Best of all those that are Attired and Clothed,

وَمُجَلِّي الْعَمَىٰ،

And the Illuminator of the Blind,

الَّذِي يَـمْلَاءُ الْأَرْضَ عَدْلًا وَقِسْطًا،

The One who will fill the Earth with justice and equity,

كَمَا مُلِئَتْ ظُلْمًا وَجَوْرًا.

Just as it was filled with injustice and oppression.

إِنَّكَ عَلَىٰ كُلِّ شَيْءٍ قَدِيرٌ.

Surely, You have Power over all things.

أَللّٰهُمَّ صَلِّ عَلَىٰ وَلِيِّكَ وَابْنِ أَوْلِيَآئِكَ،

O Allah, send Your blessings upon Your close friend, and the son of Your close friends,

أَلَّذِينَ فَرَضْتَ طَاعَتَهُمْ،

Those whom You have ordered (us) to obey,

وَأَوْجَبْتَ حَقَّهُمْ،

And You made (the observation of) their rights compulsory,

وَأَذْهَبْتَ عَنْهُمُ الرِّجْسَ وَطَهَّرْتَـهُمْ تَطْهِيراً.

And You removed from them all uncleanliness and purified them with a thorough purification.

أَللّـهُمَّ انْصُرْهُ وَانْـتَصِرْ بِهِ لِدِيـنِكَ،

O Allah, help him and come to the aid of Your Religion through him,

وَانْصُرْ بِهِ أَوْلِيَآئَكَ وَأَوْلِيآئَهُ وَشِيعَتَهُ وَأَنْصارَهُ وَاجْعَلْنَا مِنْهُمْ.

And help Your close friends - (those who are) his friends, and his followers, and his helpers, and place us among them.

أَللّـهُمَّ أَعِذْهُ مِنْ شَرِّ كُلِّ بَاغٍ وَطَاغٍ، وَمِنْ شَرِّ جَمِيعِ خَلْقِكَ،

O Allah, protect him from the evil of every tyrant and despot, and from the evil of all Your creations,

وَاحْفَظْهُ مِنْ بَيْنَ يَدَيْهِ وَمِنْ خَلْفِهِ وَعَنْ يَـمِيـنِهِ وَعَنْ شِـمَالِهِ،

And grant him protection from his front, and from his back, and from his right, and from his left,

وَاحْرُسْهُ وَامْنَعْهُ مِنْ أَنْ يُوصَلَ إِلَيْهِ بِسُوءٍ.

And protect him and prevent the reaching of any evil upon him.

وَاحْفَظْ فِيهِ رَسُولَكَ وَآلَ رَسُولِكَ،

And protect Your Messenger, and the progeny of Your Messenger through him,

وَأَظْهِرْ بِهِ الْعَدْلَ،

And make justice manifest through him,

وَأَيِّدْهُ بِالنَّصْرِ،

And support him by victory,

وَانْصُرْ نَاصِرِيهِ وَاخْذُلْ خَاذِلِيهِ،

And aid his helpers, and abandon his deserters,

وَاقْصِمْ قَاصِمِيهِ وَاقْصِمْ بِهِ جَبَابِرَةَ الْكُفْرِ.

And crush his enemies and break up the forces of disbelief through him.

وَاقْتُلْ بِهِ الْكُفَّارَ وَالْمُنَافِقِينَ وَجَمِيعَ الْمُلْحِدِينَ،

And through him, kill the disbelievers, and the hypocrites, and all the infidels,

حَيْثُ كَانُوا مِنْ مَشَارِقِ الْأَرْضِ وَمَغَارِبِهَا بَرِّهَا وَبَحْرِهَا.

Wherever they are - in the east of the Earth or its west, its land or its sea.

وَامْلَأْ بِهِ الْأَرْضَ عَدْلًا وَأَظْهِرْ بِهِ دِينَ نَبِيِّكَ صَلَّى اللهُ عَلَيْهِ وَآلِهِ.

And fill the Earth with justice through him, and manifest the religion of Your Prophet, blessings be upon him and his progeny (through him).

وَاجْعَلْنِي اللّٰهُمَّ مِنْ أَنْصَارِهِ وَأَعْوَانِهِ وَأَتْبَاعِهِ وَشِيعَتِهِ.

And place me, O Allah, among his helpers, and his aides, and his followers, and his partisans.

وَأَرِنِي فِي آلِ مُحَمَّدٍ عَلَيْهِمُ السَّلَامُ مَا يَأْمُلُونَ،

And show me in the progeny of Muḥammad, peace be upon them, whatever they are hoping for,

وَفِي عَدُوِّهِمْ مَا يَحْذَرُونَ،

And in their enemies whatever they (the enemies) are afraid of,

إِلٰهَ الْحَقِّ آمِينَ.

O Lord of the Truth, [please] accept *(Amīn).*

يَا ذَا الْجَلَالِ وَالْإِكْرَامِ يَا أَرْحَمَ الرَّاحِمِينَ.

O the Possessor of Splendour and Honour! O the Most Merciful of all those who show mercy.

Munājāt al-Manẓūmah

Introduction to Munājāt al-Manẓūmah

The Versified Whispered Prayer

Author: Anonymous

It had been a dream for at least four years to be able to translate this poetic supplication, which I first heard quite by chance, but fell in love with immediately. Upon finding the full text, translating it (and others like it) became a life goal, partly to rise to the challenge of translating such a text; and partly to allow others to understand and appreciate some measure of the eloquence of the Arabic language, which remains the primary language of the corpus of codified Islamic Supplications.

Munājāt al-Manẓūmah consists of thirty verses, all of which end in the same syllable (عْ). It was composed about fourteen centuries ago by ʿAlī ibn Abī Ṭālib ﷺ, the cousin and son-in-law of the Prophet of Islam ﷺ, and the rightful successor of the final Messenger ﷺ. As such, it contains words and phrases that are characteristic of the time and eloquence of the author and are thus characteristically challenging to render into a translation. A few aspects that I want to highlight are the following:

1. Some words and phrases are not in common use in the Arabic language today, although they may still be found in poetry.
2. There are words and verses that refer to particular religious ideas, which may not be entirely clear from a literal translation of the text and would need

clarification for a non-Muslim and/or non-Arabic speaking person.

3. Poetic license has allowed phrasal constructions that are admirably succinct in conveyance of their message, as well as a fluid word order that is not usually employed in ordinary writing. Combined with the use of words that can have more than one interpretation (more so in a poem), and with the fact that even familiar Arabic words may have a semantic field different from their literal equivalents in English, translation becomes even more challenging.
4. The imagery and metaphors used in the poem powerfully reinforce the ideas presented and skillfully enhance the mood of petitioning for greater proximity to Allah ﷻ. However, a literal translation of these metaphors would not always make equal sense in English and therefore require further explanation. In such instances, I have tried to concisely clarify the intent of the verse.

All these factors seem to have resisted translation into English so far, and I was unable to find an adequate English translation, or even a critique, to assist me. (I had to resort to an Urdu translation, which I did not find satisfactorily precise.) The translator's eternal dilemma remained - how much fidelity to maintain to the source text, and how much deviation from the original would be acceptable. I have tried my best to remain faithful to the original text, usually at the expense of the form of the passage (although some couplets do follow some sort of minimal rhyme scheme), because my target audience is one who will appreciate as literal a translation as possible. On the other hand, I have also tried to ensure that the translation flows comfortably and is stylistically English, even if read in isolation from the original text.

Before discussing these aspects in more detail however, the first dilemma that presented itself was the word which begins 90% of the verses - that being: إلهي, for which a literal rendition would be 'My God.' But the irreverent, exclamatory connotations of the English phrase made it entirely unsuitable in this context. After toying with 'My Allah' - which is also quite literal, but rather awkward-sounding in English - I finally settled on the familiar 'O Allah' despite its departure from the Arabic word's explicit (and by virtue of repetition, insistent) intimacy.

Returning to the four aspects mentioned above, I will provide two examples to illustrate each point, although there are more to be found in the text. I count each two lines of the poem as one verse and have numbered them accordingly. Both lines of the relevant verse are quoted as examples for each of the aspects discussed below.

1. Words and Phrases Used

(a) Verse 19:

إِلٰـهِي أَنِلْنِـي مِنْكَ رَوْحًا وَرَاحَةً
فَلَسْتُ سِوىٰ أَبْوَابِ فَضْلِكَ أَقْرَعُ

This verse contains the word رَوح, which depending on the context, can be synonymous with either راحة - 'ease, tranquility;' or رحمة - 'mercy.' Both meanings were found in *Al-Ghani*, the <u>lone</u> dictionary that lists the word رَوح. In the context, I felt that both would be equally valid interpretations, and I have used the word 'peace,' indicating synonymy with راحة, and to prevent a repetition of the word 'mercy,' which is used in the second line of the translated verse.

(b) Verse 21:

إِلٰـهِي حَلِيفُ الْـحُبِّ فِي اللَّيْلِ سَاهِرٌ
يُنَاجِي وَيَدْعُو وَالْمُغَفَّلُ يَهْجَعُ

This verse contains the phrase حليف الحبّ. The word حليف is not in common usage in Modern Standard Arabic, and again, *Al-Ghani* was the only dictionary that listed the word as containing the elements of meaning implied in the poem: مَنْ يَلْزَمُهُ وَلاَ يُفَارِقُهُ فِي كُلِّ الحَالاَتِ. Accordingly, I have rendered the phrase into English as 'drowned in love.'

2. Specific Religious Context

(a) Verse 1:

لَكَ الْـحَمْدُ يَا ذَا الْـجُودِ وَالْمَجْدِ
وَالْعُلىٰ تَبَارَكْتَ تُعْطِي مَنْ تَشَآءُ وَتَمْنَعُ

This verse ends with the word تمنع, which literally means 'to prevent or prohibit something.' To a Muslim, there are rationalizations for why Allah ﷻ may not grant something to them, perhaps despite their asking for it, etc. But if not considered from a religious viewpoint, God should not be the One who does not grant desires. Also, translating it into English as 'refuse,' 'prevent,' 'prohibit,' or anything similar, sounds not only incomplete (without a subject, which is unnecessary, therefore, absent in the Arabic verse), but also a strange method of praising Allah ﷻ. In the translation, I finally decided upon 'withhold' as a word with fewer negative connotations (e.g., as in withhold judgement, withhold punishment, etc.).

(b) Verse 8:

إِلٰـهِي فَآنِسْنِي بِتَلْقِينِ حُجَّتِي إِذَا كَانَ لِي فِي الْقَبْرِ مَثْوَى وَمَضْجَعُ

This verse contains the word حُجَّة which means 'proof, argument' (among other things). In Islamic terms, this word can refer to the proofs of Allah ﷻ that we cannot deny, such as the sending of Prophets to guide people, etc. It can also refer to the record of our deeds which we will not be able to deny after our death, regardless of how much we may want to. [I have understood this from the translations and/or commentaries of other supplications.] This verse also mentions تلقين which means 'instruction, teaching,' as well as being the name of the prayer which is recited at the grave of a person being buried, in which the corpse is 'reminded' about the tenets of the Islamic belief (one God – Allah; the Prophets, etc.) before one being questioned in the grave. Although the latter concept may not be explicitly meant by this word, the idea of that prayer is still evoked because of the second line of this verse which mentions the grave. However, literally translating the first verse into something akin to "Comfort me with instructions of the ultimate proofs" would sound peculiar to say the least. I modified the translation to "Let knowledge of the (ultimate) proofs accompany me," which sounds slightly more reasonable - linguistically, stylistically, and religiously, although it is not literal. Maintaining a literal paraphrase would require some amount of explanation somewhere, even for a reader who is familiar with the Islamic concepts, but I wanted to avoid having verbosity distract the reader.

3. Poetic License

I have mentioned several aspects of poetic license in the main point above, but the scope of this short commentary restricts my illustrations to two: The first one highlights eloquence in succinctness, and the second one exemplifies fluid word order.

(a) Verse 23:

إِلـٰهِي يُمَنِّينِـي رَجَآئِـي سَلاَمَةً وَقُبْحُ خَطِيئَاتِـي عَلَيَّ يُشَنِّعُ

In the second line of this verse, قُبح which means 'ugliness,' is synonymous (in idea, but not in form) with the final word يشنّع which literally means 'to make ugly.' شنّع على on the other hand, as a phrase, means 'to vilify, to libel.' The play on words deliberately serves to enhance the feeling of regret over one's misdeeds. Accordingly, the second line of this verse literally translates into something like "And the ugliness of my sins vilifies me." However, the translation does not entirely relate to the first line of the verse: "My hopes have allowed me to desire amnesty" (although the correlation is clear in Arabic). I have therefore modified the rendition of the latter half of the verse to "While the ugliness of my sins have held me back," to maintain its link to the former half.

(b) Verse 5:

إِلٰـهِي تَرىٰ حَالِي وَفَقْرِي وَفَاقَتِي وَأَنْتَ مُنَاجَاتِي الـخَفِيَّةَ تَسْمَعُ

The usual word order in Arabic sentences is Verb-Subject-Object-Adverbial, and other matter (Haywood and Nahmad, *A New Arabic Grammar*). However, in this verse, although the first line follows the usual order, the second line inverts the order and places the verb at the end to maintain the rhyme scheme in the poem. This is seen in several places in this poem (notably, verses: 4, 10, 11, 12, 14, 16, 18, 20, 21, 22, 23, 24), and is used for emphasis (also seen in the Quran, e.g., Sūrah al-Fātiḥa, verse 4, among other places). Fortunately, this feature on its own was of no great hindrance to the translation.

4. Imagery and Metaphor

(a) Verse 4:

إِلٰهِي لَئِنْ أَعْطَيْتُ نَفْسِي سُؤْلَـهَا فَهَا أَنَا فِي رَوْضِ النَّدَامَةِ أَرْتَعُ

This verse employs imagery to a great effect to drive home the idea of the undesirability to always following one's desires. The first line hypothesizes complete indulgence to whim, but the second appreciates that behaviour like this, more often than not, only brings about regret, through the use of metaphor. The line:

فَهَا أَنَا فِي رَوْضِ النَّدَامَةِ أَرْتَعُ

I would find myself lost in the land of regret

uses the word روض rather than simply أرض - *land* although the two can be considered synonymous. This is noteworthy in that روض semantically includes the idea of 'garden,' so the line suggests the incongruous image of a field that should be beautifully verdant, but which is instead reaping a distasteful harvest in one's soul and life. However, I was unable to find an English word that contains the same shade of meaning and I retained *land of regret* in the translation.

(b) Verse 16:

إِلٰهِي ذُنُوبِي بَذَّتِ الطَّوْدَ وَاعْتَلَتْ
وَصَفْحُكَ عَنْ ذَنْبِي أَجَلُّ وَأَرْفَعُ

This verse, appearing in the middle of the poem, reiterates the central theme of the supplication - asking Allah ﷻ for forgiveness of our sins. The accumulation of misdeeds is compared to the formation of mountains, *or even higher* (واعتلت), but Allah's mercy and forgiveness is described as *far greater and loftier* (أجل و أرفع). Also, although صفح - *pardon and forgiveness* is not usually described as being أرفع - *higher, loftier*, the usage of the comparative adjectival form goes back to the quality of mountains having majestic height which is mentioned in the first line of the verse. This metaphor was retained in the translation because the word *lofty* in the English language also has 'exalted, noble' as elements of meaning, which can be used to describe the pardon of Allah

ﷺ. (I did not want to reuse *high* because I wanted to employ similar synonymy in translation, to emphasize the metaphor.)

I have touched upon merely a few characteristics and features of this incredibly beautiful and poetic supplication, but I do not feel that I have done justice to it in the least - neither in the translation, nor in the above commentary. However, I hope this goes some way in providing a glimpse of the eloquence that Arabic poetry and supplications contain and serves to increase our appreciation of the language of Arabic.

Munājāt al-Manẓūmah: The Versified Whispered Prayer

Translator: Anonymous

بِسْمِ اللّٰهِ الرَّحْـمٰنِ الرَّحِيمِ

In the Name of Allah, the All-Compassionate, the All-Merciful

لَكَ الْـحَمْدُ يَا ذَا الْـجُودِ وَالْمَجْدِ وَالْعُلىٰ

تَبَارَكْتَ تُعْطِي مَنْ تَشَآءُ وَتَـمْنَعُ

For You is all praise, O Possessor of Bounty, Glory, and Eminence,

Glory be to You - You grant to whosoever You will and withhold.

إِلٰـهِي وَخَلَّاقِي وَحِرْزِي وَمَوْئِـلِي

إِلَيْكَ لَدَي الْإِعْسَارِ وَالْيُسْرِ أَفْزَعُ

O Allah! My Creator, my Fortress, and my Refuge!

To You I resort, in hardship and in ease, for relief.

إِلٰـهِي لَئِنْ جَلَّتْ وَجَمَّتْ خَطِيئَتِي

فَعَفْوُكَ عَنْ ذَنْبِي أَجَلُّ وَأَوْسَعُ

O Allah! Even if my mistakes have become grave and numerous,
Then Your Forgiveness is far greater (than those sins) and is limitless.

إِلٰهِي لَئِنْ أَعْطَيْتُ نَفْسِي سُؤْلَـهَا

فَهَا أَنَا فِي رَوْضِ النَّدَامَةِ أَرْتَعُ

O Allah! If I had given my soul all that it desired,
Then there I would be, lost in the land of regret!

إِلٰـهِي تَرىٰ حَالِي وَفَقْرِي وَفَاقَتِي

وَأَنْتَ مُنَاجَاتِي الـخَفِيَّةَ تَسْمَعُ

O Allah! You see my position, my poverty, and my destitution;
And You hear my softly whispered supplication.

إِلٰـهِي فَلاَ تَقْطَعْ رَجَآئِي وَلاَ تُزِغْ

فُؤَادِي فَلِي فِي سَيْبِ جُودِكَ مَطْمَعُ

O Allah! So, sever not my hopes, nor distract my heart (from You),
For I pine for the bounties of Your Generosity.

إِلٰـهِي لَئِنْ خَيَّبْتَنِي أَوْ طَرَدْتَنِي
فَمَنْ ذَا الَّذِي أَرْجُو وَمَنْ ذَا أُشَفِّعُ

O Allah! If You thwart me or chase me away,
Then who can I hope from, and who can I make intercede for me?

إِلٰـهِي أَجِرْنِي مِنْ عَذَابِكَ
إِنَّنِي أَسِيرٌ ذَلِيلٌ خَآئِفٌ لَكَ أَخْضَعُ

O Allah! Keep me (away) from Your punishment,
Indeed I am captive, abased, fearful, and subservient to You.

إِلٰـهِي فَآنِسْنِي بِتَلْقِينِ حُجَّتِي
إِذَا كَانَ لِي فِي الْقَبْرِ مَثْوَىً وَمَضْجَعٌ

O Allah! Let knowledge of the (ultimate) proofs accompany me,
When my grave becomes my abode and home.

إِلٰـهِي لَئِنْ عَذَّبْتَنِي أَلْفَ حِجَّةٍ
فَحَبْلُ رَجَائِي مِنْكَ لَا يَتَقَطَّعُ

O Allah! Even if You punish me for a thousand years,
My hopes in You will nonetheless never be severed.

إِلٰـهِي أَذِقْنِي طَعْمَ عَفْوِكَ يَوْمَ
لَا بَنُونَ وَلاَ مَالٌ هُنَالِكَ يَنْفَعُ

O Allah! Let me savour Your forgiveness on the Day,
When neither progeny, nor wealth will be of any avail.

إِلٰـهِي لَئِنْ لَمْ تَرْعَنِي كُنْتُ ضَآئِعًا
وَإِنْ كُنْتَ تَرْعَانِي فَلَسْتُ أُضَيَّعُ

O Allah! If you do not watch out for me, I will be lost!
But since You do watch over me, I am never lost.

إِلٰـهِي إِذَا لَمْ تَعْفُ عَنْ غَيْرِ مُـحْسِنٍ
فَمَنْ لِمُسِيءٍ بِالهَوىٰ يَتَمَتَّعُ

O Allah! If You do not forgive any but the doers of good,
Then who is there for the disobedient, who indulge in their desires?

إِلٰـهِي لَئِنْ فَرَّطْتُ فِي طَلَبِ التُّقىٰ
فَهَا أَنَا إِثْرَ الْعَفْوِ أَقْفُو وَأَتْبَعُ

O Allah! Even though I have been negligent in pursuing goodness,
I am now tracing and following the path to forgiveness.

إِلٰـهِي لَئِنْ أَخْطَأْتُ جَهْلًا فَطَالَـمَا

رَجَوْتُكَ حَتّٰى قِيلَ مَا هُوَيَـجْزَعُ

O Allah! I may have sinned in ignorance, but I have also always,

Hoped (for Your Grace), until others wondered if I ever worried (about rejection).

إِلٰـهِي ذُنُوبِي بَذَّتِ الطَّوْدَ وَاعْتَلَتْ

وَصَفْحُكَ عَنْ ذَنْبِي أَجَلُّ وَأَرْفَعُ

O Allah! My sins have become mountains or even higher,

But Your capacity for pardon is far greater and loftier.

إِلٰـهِي يُنَحِّي ذِكْرُ طَوْلِكَ لَوْعَتِـي

وَذِكْرُ الْـخَطَايَا الْعَيْنَ مِنِّي يُدَمِّعُ

O Allah! Remembrance of Your Might alleviates my sorrows,

While remembrance of my mistakes makes my eyes shed tears.

إِلٰـهِي أَقِلْنِي عَثْرَتِي وَامْحُ حَوْبَتِي

فَإِنِّي مُقِرٌّ خَآئِفٌ مُتَضَرِّعُ

O Allah! Reduce my lapses and efface my sins,

For (here) I am confessing, fearful, and beseeching.

إِلٰـهِي أَنِلْنِـي مِنْكَ رَوْحًا وَرَاحَةً

فَلَسْتُ سِوىٰ أَبْوَابِ فَضْلِكَ أَقْرَعُ

O Allah! Grant me peace from You, and tranquillity,
For I knock but at the gates of Your Mercy.

إِلٰـهِي لَئِنْ أَقْصَيْتَنِـي أَوْ أَهَنْتَنِـي

فَمَا حِيلَتِـي يَا رَبِّ أَمْ كَيْفَ أَصْنَعُ

O Allah! If You distance me from Yourself or debase me,
Then what recourse do I have, O Lord - what would I do?

إِلٰـهِي حَلِيفُ الْـحُبِّ فِي اللَّيْلِ سَاهِرٌ

يُنَاجِي وَيَدْعُو وَالْمُغَفَّلُ يَهْجَعُ

O Allah! Those drowned in (Your) love remain awake all night,
Entreating and praying (to You), while the unmindful slumber.

إِلٰـهِي وَهٰذَا الْـخَلْقُ مَا بَيْنَ نَائِمٍ

وَمُنْتَبِهٍ فِي لَيْلِهِ يَتَضَرَّعُ

O Allah! Here are creatures, most of whom are asleep,
But the mindful use their nights to supplicate to You.

وكُلُّهُمْ يَرجُونَوَالَكَ رَاجِيًا

لِرَحْـمَتِكَ الْعُظْمىٰ وَفِي الْـخُلْدِ يَطْمَعُ

But all of them hope for Your Favours, and remain hopeful,
Of Your Infinite Mercy, and of a Heaven eternal.

إِلٰـهِي يُـمَنِّينِـي رَجَآئِـي سَلاَمَةً

وَقُبْحُ خَطِيئَاتِـي عَلَيَّ يُشَنِّعُ

O Allah! My hopes have allowed me to desire amnesty,
While the ugliness of my sins has held me back.

إِلٰـهِي فَإِنْ تَعْفُوفَعَفْوُكَ مُنْقِذِي

وَإِلَّا فَبِالذَّنْبِ الْمُدَمِّرِ أُصْرَعُ

O Allah! So, if You forgive me, then Your Pardon will save me,
Else I will be destroyed by my devastating misdeeds.

إِلٰـهِي بِـحَقِّ الْـهَاشِمِيِّ مُـحَمَّدٍ

وَحُرْمَةِ أَطْهَارٍ هُمُ لَكَ خُضَّعٌ

O Allah! For the sake of the Hashimite Muḥammad,
And the sacredness of the Purified (Ones) who humble themselves before You.

إِلٰـهِي بِـحَقِّ الْمُصْطَفىٰ وَابْنِ عَمِّهِ

وَحُرْمَةِ أَبْرَارٍ هُمُ لَكَ خُشَّعُ

O Allah! For the sake of Muṣṭafā and his cousin (Imam ʿAlī عليه السلام),
And the sanctity of the virtuous (ones) who truly submit to You.

إِلٰـهِي فَأَنْشِرْنِـي عَلٰى دِينِ أَحْمَدٍ

مُنِيبًا تَقِيًّا قَانِتًا لَكَ أَخْضَعُ

O Allah! Resurrect me as a follower of the religion of Aḥmad,
And as a repentant, devout, obedient, and humble (servant) to You.

وَلاَ تَـحْرِمَنِّـي يَا إِلٰـهِي وَسَيِّدِي

شَفَاعَتَهُ الْكُبْرىٰ فَذٰاكَ الْمُشَفَّعُ

And do not deny me, O my Allah, O my Master,
His noble intercession, for he is the (perfect) mediator.

وَصَلِّ عَلَيْهِمْ مَا دَعَاكَ مُوَحِّدٌ

وَنَاجَاكَ أَخْيَارٌ بِبَابِكَ رُكَّعٌ

And bless him whenever a Monotheist calls upon You,
And whenever the righteous bow at Your door, beseeching You.

اللهم صل على محمد وآل محمد وعجل فرجهم

O Allah! Send Your blessings upon Muḥammad and the Family of Muḥammad, and hasten their relief

Other Publications Available[32]

1. *A Land Most Goodly: The Story of Yemen in the Quran and in the Times of Prophet Muḥammad and Imam ʿAlī ibn Abī Ṭālib,* by Jaffer Ladak
2. *A Star Amongst the Stars: The Life and Times of the Great Companion: Jabir ibn Abdullah al-Ansari,* by Jaffer Ladak*
3. *Alif, Baa, Taa of Kerbala,* by Saleem Bhimji and Arifa Hudda
4. *Arbāʿīn of Imam Ḥusayn,* compiled and translated by Saleem Bhimji
5. *Daily Devotions,* compiled and translated by Saleem Bhimji*
6. *Deficient? A Review of Sermon 80 from Nahj al-Balāgha,* by Āyatullāh al-ʿUẓmā Shaykh Nāṣir Makārim Shīrāzī and translated by Saleem Bhimji
7. *Exegesis of the 29th Juz of the Quran - a Translation of Tafsīr Nemunah,* by Āyatullāh al-ʿUẓmā Shaykh Nāṣir Makārim Shīrāzī and translated by Saleem Bhimji*
8. *Foundations of Islamic Unity* - a translation of *Al-Fuṣūl al-Muhimmah fī Taʾlīf al-Ummah,* by ʿAbd al-Ḥusayn Sharaf al-Dīn al-Mūsawī al-ʿĀmilī and translated by Batool Ispahany*

---

[32] The following is a list of all the original writings and translations from the Islamic Publishing House. As many of these titles are out of stock, we are slowly re-releasing all our works via Print-on-Demand through Amazon.

Titles with an * after the name are currently available via Amazon from their international platforms, including Australia, Canada, France, Germany, Italy, Japan, UK, USA, Netherlands, and Spain.

If you cannot find any of the above titles on Amazon, feel free to email us at **iph@iph.ca**.

9. *Fountain of Paradise - Fāṭima az-Zahrā᾽ in the Noble Quran,* by Āyatullāh al-ʿUẓmā Shaykh Nāṣir Makārim Shīrāzī, compiled and translated by Saleem Bhimji*
10. *God and god of Science,* by Syed Hasan Raza Jafri*
11. *House of Sorrows,* by Shaykh ʿAbbās al-Qummī and translated by Aejaz Ali Turab Husayn Husayni*
12. *Iʿtikāf: The Spiritual Retreat – The Philosophy, Spiritual Mysteries and Practical Rulings,* compiled and translated by Saleem Bhimji*
13. *Inspirational Insights,* by Mohammed Khaku
14. *Islam and Religious Pluralism,* by Āyatullāh Shaykh Murtaḍā Muṭahharī and translated by Sayyid Sulayman Ali Hasan
15. *Journey to Eternity - A Handbook of Supplications for the Soul,* compiled and translated by Saleem Bhimji and Arifa Hudda*
16. *Love and Hate for Allah's Sake,* by Mujtaba Saburi translated by Saleem Bhimji
17. *Love for the Family,* compiled and translated by Yasin T. Al-Jibouri, Saleem Bhimji, and others
18. *Moral Management,* by Abbas Rahimi and translated by Saleem Bhimji*
19. *Morals of the Masumeen,* by Arifa Hudda
20. *Prayers of the Final Prophet - A Collection of Supplications of Prophet Muḥammad,* by ʿAllāmah Sayyid Muḥammad Ḥusayn Ṭabā᾽ṭabā᾽ī and translated by Tahir Ridha-Jaffer*
21. *Prospering Through a Cost of Living Crisis,* by Jaffer Ladak*
22. *Ramaḍān Reflections,* compiled by A Group of Muslim Scholars and translated by Saleem Bhimji*
23. *Ṣalāt al-Āyāt,* by Saleem Bhimji

24. *Ṣalāt al-Ghufaylah: Salvation through Patience & Perseverance,* written by Saleem Bhimji*
25. *Ṣalāt al-Jumuʿah - History, Philosophy, 40 Ahadith on the Importance of Various Ṣalāt, and Practical Rulings,* according to the rulings of Āyatullāh Sayyid ʿAlī al-Ḥusaynī al-Sīstānī, compiled and translated by Saleem Bhimji
26. *Secrets of the Ḥajj,* by Āyatullāh al-ʿUẓmā Shaykh Ḥusayn Mazāherī and translated by Saleem Bhimji
27. *Sunan an-Nabī,* by ʿAllāmah Sayyid Muḥammad Ḥusayn Ṭabāʾṭabāʾī and translated by Tahir Ridha-Jaffer
28. *Tears from Heaven's Flowers: An Anthology of English Poetry about the Ahlulbayt,* by Abrahim al-Zubeidi
29. *The Day the Germs Caused Fitnah,* by Umm Maryam*
30. *The Firmest Armament: Commentary on Āyatul Kursī (The Verse of the Throne),* by Sayyid Nasrullah Burujerdi and translated by Saleem Bhimji*
31. *The Last Luminary and Ways to Delve into the Light,* by Sayyid Muḥammad Ridha Husayni Mutlaq and translated by Saleem Bhimji*
32. *The Muslim Legal Will Booklet,* by Saleem Bhimji*
33. *The Pure Life,* by Āyatullāh al-ʿUẓmā as-Sayyid Muḥammad Taqī al-Modarresī and translated by Jaffer Ladak with commentary by Dr. Zainali Panjwani and Jaffer Ladak*
34. *The Third Testimony: Imam ʿAlī in the Adhān,* compiled and translated by Saleem Bhimji*
35. *The Tragedy of Kerbalāʾ,* as narrated by Imam ʿAlī ibn al-Ḥusayn al-Sajjād (a), recorded by Shaykh al-Ṣadūq and translated by ʿAbdul Zahrāʾ ʿAbdul Ḥusayn*
36. *The Torch of Perpetual Guidance - A Brief Commentary on*

Ziyārat al-ʿĀshūrāʾ, by ʿAbbās Azizi and translated by Saleem Bhimji

37. *Weapon of the Believer*, by ʿAllāmah Muḥammad Bāqir Majlisī and translated by Saleem Bhimji*

Upcoming Publications

1. *Beyond the 40ᵗʰ: Understanding the Exclusive Significance of the Arbaʿīn of Imam al-Ḥusayn* 🕌, by the late Āyatullāh al-Sayyid Muḥammad Muḥsin Ḥusaynī Ṭehrānī, translated by Saleem Bhimji

2. *Guided By Faith: The Islamic Management Model*, written by ʿAbbās Raḥīmī, translated by Saleem Bhimji

3. *Khums: The Fiscal Blueprint for Community Self-Sufficiency*, by Saleem Bhimji

4. *Knocking on Heaven's Doors*, compiled with translations by Saleem Bhimji

5. *Propaganda and Piety: The Umayyad Rewriting of Syria [From Historical Syria to Apocalyptic Syria]*, written by Shaykh Rasūl Jaʿfariyān, translated by Saleem Bhimji

6. *Ramaḍān Devotions - A Collection of Supplications for the Nights of Qadr*, compiled with translations by Saleem Bhimji

7. *Blessed Desires: Islamic Perspectives on Sexuality and the Soul*, by ʿAlī Ḥoseinzādeh, translated by Saleem Bhimji

8. *Shadows of Dissent*, by Āyatullāh Shaykh Nāṣir Makārim Shīrāzī, translated by Saleem Bhimji and the Translator's Guild of the Islamic Publishing House

9. *Supplication for the People of the Frontiers*, by Shaykh Ḥusayn Anṣāriān, translated by Saleem Bhimji

10. *The Arbaʿīn: A look into the Ziyārat of Arbaʿīn*, written by Saleem Bhimji
11. *The Comprehensive Book of Marriage and Divorce Formulas*, by Saleem Bhimji
12. *The Young Muslims Daily Devotions Manuals - Volumes I and II*, compiled and translated by Saleem Bhimji
13. *Victor Not Victim: A Biography of Lady Zaynab bint ʿAlī along with 200 Short Stories About Her Life*, researched and written by Saleem Bhimji

In addition to the above, our *Living the Quran Through The Living Quran* series of commentary on the Noble Quran is also being published. To date, we have released the commentary of:

1. Sūrah Qāf (50)
2. Sūrah al-Najm (53)
3. Sūrah al-Mujādilah (58)

The commentary of the following chapters of the Quran will also be released in the future:

1. Sūrah al-Fātiḥa (1)
2. Sūrah Yāsīn (36)
3. Sūrah al-Wāqiʿah (56)
4. Sūrah al-Ṣaff (61)

If you would like to donate to any of our ongoing projects, whether the books, videos, or other publications, you can contribute in the following ways:

1. **Within Canada:** Send an e-transfer from your Canadian bank account to **iph@iph.ca**
2. **International:** Send your transfer via PayPal to **saleem1176@rogers.com**

For more information, contact us at **iph@iph.ca**

www.ingramcontent.com/pod-product-compliance
Lightning Source LLC
LaVergne TN
LVHW011349080426
835511LV00005B/201
* 9 7 8 1 9 2 7 9 3 0 5 4 0 *